# *A Love Letter*
## to My Children

No matter how difficult the circumstances,
there is always hope for a brighter future.

## EVE JOHNSTON

A Love Letter to My Children
©2020 Eve Johnston

All rights reserved. This book or parts thereof may not be reproduced in any form, stored in a retrieval system, or transmitted in any form by any means – electronic, mechanical, photocopy, recording or otherwise – without prior written permission of the author, except as provided by Australian copyright law.

Unless otherwise stated, Scripture quotations are taken from the New King James Version®. Copyright © 1982 by Thomas Nelson. Used by permission. All rights reserved.

Author's Disclaimer: I have tried to recreate events, locales and conversations from my memories of them. To protect privacy, in some instances I have changed the names of individuals. I have made every effort to ensure that the information in this book is correct and do not assume and hereby disclaim any liability to any party for any loss, damage, or disruption in the event of errors or omissions or if they should disagree with the inclusion of the content herein.

**Cover Design:** Laureth Rumble, Pumpkin Island, Queensland, Australia

**Edit and Interior Design**: Carol Martinez

### Author's Contact Information:

www.evejohnston.com
eve@evejohnston.com

ISBN: 978-0-646-82798-8
Published in Australia

*This book is dedicated to ...*

My dear family whom I love with all my heart,
and to my mum and dad for their faith-filled prayers

# *Endorsement*

Yvonne's beautiful storytelling and courageous vulnerability paints a picture of how the presence of Jesus Christ intersects with the brokenness of childhood trauma and immense suffering. This book highlights the power of Redemptive Grace woven through a lifetime of trauma. This story of hope is an inspirational account of how Jesus restores what suffering has destroyed.

*Jacqueline King*
Trauma and Family Counsellor

# Contents

Foreword ..... 9

Introduction ..... 13

Chapter 1—The early days (1952-1957) ..... 17

Chapter 2—Lynne and me (1957-1964) ..... 27

Chapter 3—Close call in our farm creek (1964) ..... 36

Chapter 4—My first place of employment (1964-1967) ..... 40

Chapter 5—Shattered dreams (1967-1969) ..... 49

Chapter 6—The home for unmarried mothers (1969-1970) ..... 56

Chapter 7—The birth of my son (1970) ..... 62

Chapter 8—In search of truth (1970-1978) ..... 69

Chapter 9—Domestic Violence (1978-1980) ..... 78

Chapter 10—Domestic violence *continued* ..... 88

Chapter 11—A glimpse of hope (1980) ..... 95

Chapter 12—Deception (1980-1982) ..... 103

Chapter 13—The power of forgiveness (1982-1983) ..... 112

Chapter 14—Alternative lifestyle (1983-1985) ..... 118

Chapter 15—City life (1985-1988) ..... 127

Chapter 16—Obsession, dysfunction & heartache (1988-1998) ..... 140

Chapter 17—Roller coaster ride (1998-2001) ..... 150

Chapter 18—Running from God (2001-2007) ..... 156

Chapter 19—Another miraculous healing (2007-2010) ..... 160

Chapter 20—The simple believes every word (2010-2012) ..... 166

Chapter 21—Revelation (2012-2013) ..... 176

Chapter 22—Reaching out to the lost (2013) ..... 180

Chapter 23—They will lay hands on the sick (2013-2014) ..... 193

Chapter 24—How I found my son (1970-2016) ..... 206

Chapter 25—A dream come true (2016) ..... 215

Chapter 26—Discovering your identity in Christ Jesus ..... 221

Chapter 27—A love letter from God ..... 228

Epilogue ..... 237

# Foreword

Once it was the blessing, Now it is the Lord;
Once it was the feeling, Now it is His Word.
Once His gifts I wanted, Now the Giver own;
Once I sought for healing, Now Himself alone.
Once I hoped in Jesus, Now I know He's mine;
Once my lamps were dying, Now they brightly shine.
Once for death I waited, Now His coming hail;
And my hopes are anchored, Safe within the veil.

A. B. Simpson

'All glory to God'. This is the declaration uttered by Eve Johnston daily. Her desire is that the sharing of her life story through this book will 'bring glory to God'.

Eve has been a close friend of our family for the past ten years. I shall never forget the first time I met this striking lady with the tender eyes. She walked into the Sunday School class with her beautiful granddaughter. I remember being drawn to her as a loving mother figure. Her love for children was evident in the way she related to their innocence and vulnerability.

Over the years we have grown very close to Eve and it was with great excitement that she returned from a mission trip to Mozambique and announced that God had clearly asked her to write a book of her life's journey.

This book is inspired as Eve spent hours and hours, days and days, on her own, sometimes on Pumpkin Island off the coast of Yeppoon, Australia —listening, waiting, recording life events and asking the Holy Spirit to give her the correct words to write.

During this time, God, through the Holy Spirit, allowed her to revisit aspects of her life, past hurts, failures, accomplishments and to see the miraculous. It was in the dark moments where she saw the Grand Weaver—our Heavenly Father, weaving a magnificent tapestry that even Eve could not believe was possible.

As you read this book you will see that this is not only Eve's life journey, but a journey of God's power, God's majesty, God's supernatural intervention and God causing all things to work for the good of those who love Him and are called according to His purpose.

Eve's life story is a testament of obedience and the protection of our loving Heavenly Father. She has experienced rejection, pain, suffering, and making big decisions on her own. She has also encountered the joy that comes in the morning, while wearing a garment of praise.

Eve, like so many others, faced personal battles, personal pain and struggles. It is only through God's grace, His love, His mercy through Jesus our Saviour, that Eve has risen above all these trials and adversities and has become a Godly woman, a Godly mother, a Godly grandmother, a Godly great-grandmother and a true Godly friend.

You will not only be inspired and encouraged when you read this book, but I am sure you will experience healing and blessing as you

## FOREWORD

see God's miraculous work in the life of an ordinary sinner like me and you.

To Eve's son, daughters, grandchildren, family and friends all over the world. May God use this book to encourage you, heal you, show you His Love and shine light in the darkness you experience.

Eve's biggest desire is that you will experience the love of God our Father, His grace, mercy and peace through JESUS CHRIST our Saviour and the communion of the Holy Spirit. We can only be forgiven, healed and reconciled back to God by placing our faith in JESUS CHRIST and starting a personal relationship with Him. It does not matter what you have done or how far away you feel from God. You can have Him in your life right now.

*Corné, Natalie, Danae and Stefan Esterhuysen*

**The Spirit and the Bride say,
'Come, Lord JESUS. come'.**

*Revelation 22:12*

*P.S. Eve — Thank you for your obedience — The devil has no hold on you – the blood of JESUS has set you free*

# Introduction

**To my dear children,**

I am writing this letter to explain a few things that I may not have mentioned to you before, and to tell you that I love you. I am sorry it has taken me until now to put pen to paper. Many times, I began to write but did not quite know how to express myself.

Your grandmother pleaded with me years ago to write my story, as she felt it was important that you know everything about my past. Many years later, in an orphanage in Mozambique, I met a man who confirmed this. He told me he had heard the exact same thing in a message he had received for me from God. My mum thought that my story would be beneficial to others who may be in, or have come out

'*No matter how bad circumstances may be, there is hope for a brighter future*'.

of, similar situations to what we experienced; that it would help them to realise that no matter how bad their circumstances may be, there is hope for a brighter future.

I feel it is important for you to know that my life was not all bad. I was fortunate to spend the first fourteen years on a dairy farm in the Northern Rivers of New South Wales Australia, waking each day to a new adventure. As a child, I roamed freely through lush pasture among our farm animals, feeling totally loved and accepted. My parents, although not well-off at the time, provided well for my siblings and me. It seemed I had not a care in the world until suddenly all of this changed, and my life of freedom almost ceased to be.

When I was seventeen, another significant event occurred-it impacted me in such a way that I began to live in 'fight or flight' mode. I constantly sought ways to distract myself from the heartache and pain that this experience had caused. As a number of you already know to a certain extent, the following thirty-nine years consisted of several failed marriages and other relationships, including an 18-month stint of extreme domestic violence. Through the years, I accumulated a number of addictions and obsessive disorders and dabbled in the occult. Other injustices followed; however, I gradually began to find my voice and fight for myself and also for you. I did this in a way that I felt no one had ever fought for me, mostly due to the times in which I lived.

I am so sorry for putting you through so much pain and suffering due to the unwise decisions I made at the time. I pray that you can find it in your hearts to forgive me for any hurt I may have caused you, either directly or indirectly. Even though you were with me during the good times and the bad, you might have been too young to remember, or, in order to cope, you may have erased the memories from your mind. I am eternally grateful for your grandparent's unwavering faith

## INTRODUCTION

in God, and believe that for this reason, along with their prayers, we are still alive today.

When I was fifty-six years old, my life suddenly changed for the better, when a friend introduced me to Jesus. As a child I knew of Him but did not know Him personally. Through Jesus and His love for me, I found hope and experienced peace for the first time in years.

My prayer for you is that by reading my story, you will come to an understanding that, no matter how bad things seem to be at times, there is still hope of living a life of freedom.

I pray that you are blessed as you read the following pages, and you find solace in realising just how special and loved you really are.

Love always,

*Mum* xoxo

## Chapter One

## The Early Days

### —1952-1957—

My parents met at a Fellowship meeting in Lismore, New South Wales, Australia, when they were both in their late teens. They often attended the same church camps at Shaw's Bay and ended up falling in love and marrying in March 1944. After this, they moved to Dunoon in the state of New South Wales, onto a farm owned by my father's parents. There they milked cows and raised a few pigs. Following the birth of their first daughter in 1946, my grandparents sold my father and mother the 'home farm' (which was 40 acres), for 2,500 pounds. This was apparently a lot of money back in those days.

The land was sloping and ideal for growing bananas, so my father set about breaking up the ground behind the homestead, using a team of bullocks. Once the plantation began producing, my parents packed the bananas and sent them off to market. On the farm they had a small herd of beef cattle and a few dairy cows which they milked by hand.

My mum separated the cream from the milk using a small hand separator and made butter, selling any surplus to their neighbours.

Times were certainly hard back then, and because it was wartime, Mum and Dad supplemented their farm produce with ration tickets which they used to purchase tea, petrol, sugar and clothing. The farm had a large orchard, so my mum, through necessity, became a very good jam maker and preserver of fruit. They also had chickens, which supplied enough eggs for her to make sponge cakes, slices and biscuits. The chickens themselves were a source of food for the occasional Sunday roast. My second eldest sister was born in 1948. As they grew older, these two little girls had to fill in a lot of time by themselves whilst my busy parents packed bananas and milked cows. Mum was often tired as her daily life consisted of trying to juggle farm work, looking after a huge garden and caring for two little ones, as well as completing the other daily chores.

My parents were very regular churchgoers, which was a good opportunity for them to break the routine of hard farm work. One Sunday night, (so the story goes), my dad was in church by himself. By this time Mum was pregnant with me, and on that particular evening she was feeling too tired to accompany him. The minister preached a sermon he named, 'Go through the Gate', emphasizing that an opportunity should not be missed. This message had a dramatic effect on my dad. He told Mum that it was as though God was speaking directly to him, via the minister's message.

At this point in time, the Government was urging farmers to go into dairying, as the produce from this was much needed in Australia and overseas. So, recalling the message my dad heard at church, and seeing this as maybe the opportunity God had spoken of, my parents began looking for a dairy farm. They fell in love with one at a place called Mullumbimby, which was to be auctioned within a few weeks.

The property was ideal as it was connected to the town water supply, meaning there would be less concern if they were ever faced with a drought. Even though the farm was in the country, it was not far from a small township and schools. My father purchased the property at auction, sold the 'home farm' back to my grandfather and the family moved approximately six weeks prior to my birth. It was a beautiful dairy farm with rolling hills, green pastures and a tree lined creek which meandered its way along the boundary.

I was born on the 22nd May, 1952, at the Mullumbimby hospital. When I was three days old, I became very ill and after further testing, doctors discovered that I was suffering with a Vitamin K deficiency, which caused me to haemorrhage from the bowel. Mum and I were transported by ambulance to a larger, more specialised hospital in the area. It was touch and go for a few days. I required a blood transfusion, but it was a weekend and the blood needed to be transported from Sydney – a good nine hours via road. I almost lost my life because of the long wait. Finally, the transfusion was performed by the only doctor in the district capable of giving new babies transfusions through an ankle vein, an art he had learnt in England. In my mother's own words, 'she never looked back'. I guess she meant that after such a precarious start to life, I had a fairly healthy childhood.

My earliest memories of life on our farm are very vivid. I can remember myself as a three-year-old, steadying buckets of fresh warm milk for our baby calves that had been weaned from their mothers. I had to hold the buckets firmly, so the little calves did not knock them over, as they sometimes bunted the side of the bucket in the same manner as when suckling from their mothers. In order to teach them to drink, I placed my hand in the bucket, coated it with milk, offered my hand to the baby calf to suck, then gradually drew my hand towards the bucket. I loved the feeling of their rough little tongues as they sucked strongly on my hand.

In 1956, my mum gave birth to a beautiful, blonde, curly-haired baby boy. Now we were four. I don't remember being cuddled or held very much as a young child, but I knew my parents loved me, despite the lack of physical contact. That was just how it was back then. Mum used to tell us of her strict upbringing, especially by her dad. He had lots of rules and regulations that she and her two younger brothers had to follow.

We went to Church every Sunday and attended most of the functions that the Church offered. These included Sunday school picnics, concerts and a tradition that is greatly frowned upon now within the church—Halloween, or 'celebration of harvests', as it was called back then. It was at one of these events that I first remember something 'bad' happening to me, which then continued to become a regular occurrence at almost every Church function we attended. I was very young at the time.

It all began at a Church picnic at Brunswick Heads. It was a perfect summer's day, and as the adults relaxed at picnic tables on the riverbank, the older children eagerly headed for the coolness of the water. I waited patiently for my dad to escort me. After what seemed like forever, he changed into his swimming trunks and led me by the hand to the river. When we reached the water's edge, a man known to my family, offered to take care of me. It was then that my dad, who wasn't really a fan of swimming, unknowingly handed me into the care of a paedophile. Once in the water, this man hurt me by touching me roughly in private places on my tiny body. I began to scream and beat him in the face with my fists. 'I hate you; I hate you', I recall screaming.

On hearing my frantic cries and being totally unaware of what had just taken place, my dad ran into the water and dragged me, still screaming, from the man's arms, apologizing profusely to him, for my bad behaviour. He took me to our car, where he told me I was to remain for the rest of the day. This was so confusing for me as a little girl.

What had I done wrong to deserve to be punished in this way? This was just the beginning of the sexual abuse I suffered at the hands of this man, which continued until I was eleven years old.

Life on our farm was good. Both my older sisters and I had set chores before and after school. I remember drinking warm, frothy milk from the milk vat, and sometimes I squeezed it into my mouth, straight from the cow's udder. In order to retrieve milk from the vat, I climbed a small ladder, scooped out a cup of the delectable warm beverage, and scoffed it down quickly in case I was discovered in the act. And sometimes I was. But I loved that milk so much that it was well worth receiving a red handprint on my bottom now and again. Another activity that brought me great joy was to ride the calves around the paddock. (Of course, when no one was watching.) This activity was also frowned upon by my parents and came with the guarantee that if I was caught, I would be punished in some way.

At times down in the pigsty, old mother pig gave birth to multiple piglets. They were irresistible, and they smelled so sweet. I used to lie down with my head resting on the sow's hind leg, patiently waiting until her babies had had their fill so I could play with them. How she never harmed me, I will never know.

The milk from the dairy was put through a 'separator', to separate the cream, which was then placed in cans and sent to town on a lorry, (which also doubled as our 'school bus'). My father would then pump most of the skim milk to the 'piggery' for the pigs to drink. He used to add some sort of powdered milk to the skim as a supplement, once the cream had been removed. We only ever had fresh full cream milk in the house, so one day I decided to taste the milk powder that I had discovered down in the pig sty. I fell in love with it and rated it almost as highly as a chocolate coated 'Have A Heart' ice cream.

Another food supplement my dad fed the pigs was molasses. He stored it in a drum from which he poured the required amount into a smaller open container. Often there was a tablespoon full or more of molasses left in that smaller vessel. Every time I visited the piggery, I had myself a right feast of powdered milk (which stuck like glue to the roof of my mouth,) and molasses. My feasting days came to an abrupt halt however, when one day there seemed to be a lot more than a tablespoon of molasses in the container. I had not had molasses for quite a while, so I dipped greedily into it with a cup, took a huge mouthful, and spat it straight out again. A rat obviously loved molasses too, and had become stuck in it, then died and decomposed. I had placed in my mouth molasses as well as rat fur and who knows what else. I never ate anything from the piggery again.

When my little brother was old enough, he too was introduced to taking part in the family chores along with us girls. I remember him helping me feed the calves with buckets. That was until Dad purchased a 'you-beaut' appliance called a 'calfeteria'. It consisted of a long trough with teats on the outside connected to tubes on the inside, running down into the milk which Dad poured for the calves. My brother and I became redundant in our calf-feeding job and were introduced to other chores, such as shovelling cow poo into a heap after the milking had finished. As I grew older, I learnt how to leg-rope the cows to prevent being kicked, and to prepare them for hand-milking prior to putting on the milking machines.

My younger brother and I became quite a team, especially when it came to annoying our older sisters. Our eldest began dating a boy who lived along our road and would ride his bike to our house after school most days. He and my sister would then go to her bedroom and lock the door. I used to encourage my little brother to peek through the keyhole to see what they were doing. We thought maybe they would be kissing. On hearing our stifled laughter and whispering, my sister would hang a coat over the doorknob, covering the keyhole. With that, I would find a slender stick and poke at the coat through the hole, until it fell to the floor. My eldest sister was so patient with us and if (or when) we did actually catch a glimpse of them, her male friend and she would be sitting innocently side by side, usually reading or completing homework together.

One day my brother and I became quite bored with our 'peeking' activities, so we decided to hang the poor boy's bike high up in a tree. It was quite a mission to get it up there, and we laughed and laughed at the thought of him trying to manoeuvre it back down again. It turned out that the laugh was on us. I remember with regret the sting of my mum's hand across my backside when she discovered what we had done. And, of course, she knew I was the instigator.

When I was four and a half years old, I began Primary School. I still remember the first day, terrified of being left alone in a strange place with a bunch of sniffling crying children, whom I had never met. I informed my mum that I wasn't staying and was coming home with her. As she turned to leave, I dragged behind her for a time, clinging to one corner of her full skirt. But I quickly did as I was told after receiving a hard smack. She told me to get to school and stop being a baby or else I would be given 'something else to cry about'. (A silly expression I regrettably took on and said to my own children). In no time at all, I looked forward to attending school each day.

Mornings on the farm consisted of my siblings and I doing our chores in the dairy, preparing for school, walking down the hill to the road, and waiting for our 'lift'; which just so happened to be the cream truck I spoke of earlier. Our seats were the cream cans. There were bench seats around the outside edges of the truck, but as we were almost the last children to be picked up, we rarely had the luxury of proper seating. This was quite an acceptable and normal way for us to travel while we were still in primary grades, but once we reached high school, we were teased, and at times almost bullied, about our mode of transport to and from school. I still sometimes have nightmares about that silly cream truck. I dream that I am not ready in time, and it goes to town without me.

Each Sunday we dressed in our very best clothes, (my mum, sisters and I, also wearing hats and gloves,) and headed off to church, in our FJ Holden. It was a beautiful drive along Mullumbimby Creek Road, amidst rolling green hills and deep valleys with fat cattle grazing peacefully. Up the last hill before town, past the old sawmill we went, Dad with both hands on the wheel, casually lifting his right hand to wave to an odd car or two we may happen to encounter along the way. Finally, we would arrive in the sleepy little town of Mullumbimby and at our beautiful old Presbyterian Church.

As a small child, I used to think that our Minister quite resembled a penguin, as he walked down the aisle in his black robes and white collar, just prior to beginning the service. Mum was always prepared with containers full of macadamia nuts from our own trees and homemade biscuits in her handbag, just in case we grew restless during the Church service. I found church quite boring, probably because I did not understand what was being said half the time. But as soon as the Minister spoke about 'missions', my attention was immediately drawn back to what he was talking about. Sometimes he would incorporate a slide show to fully explain what missionaries were doing in Australia and far off countries to help people in need. It somehow stirred my heart; so much so that when my mum or dad would ask me what I wanted to be when I grew up, I would always reply, 'a missionary'.

Something else I noticed about the Minister was that when he became particularly passionate about a subject, a 'glow' would appear around him. It was so dazzling that I could hardly look at it. I used to get very excited about this and try to draw Mum's attention to the fact in order to tell her. She would just look at me with pity and shake her head. I guess I was a very 'different' child. Halfway through Church, the children were released into Sunday School. Off we would go, clutching our handkerchiefs with our pennies for the offering plate tied securely in a knot in one of the corners. We sang our little hearts out to such songs as 'Hear the pennies dropping, listen as they fall, everyone for Jesus, he can have them all', and, 'Jesus loves me this I know, for the Bible tells me so'. (Little did my family, or I, know at this time, that I would be teaching this same song to an English class in an orphanage High School in Mozambique, 59 years later.)

As much as I loved Sunday School, (and church sometimes), I still approached the church social activities with great trepidation and fear in my heart. I longed to be with the other children, but I was afraid of the abuse that continued to happen to me, at the hands of the male person who took advantage of both my age and my innocence. He also took advantage of the fact that even if I told anyone about what he was doing to me, nobody believed me. So, the abuse continued. The other children would always run away when approached by this man, laughing like it was some sort of game. But because I was the smallest and youngest of the group, this despicable person could easily catch me. Each time, I would scream in pain and anger as he held me tightly and sexually abused me. This was sadly judged by others who heard the angry tirade erupting from me towards him, as my being 'disrespectful'. I was then disciplined for my 'bad behaviour'. The church events we attended at which this abuse took place were usually either at night while the other children and I played innocently around the church or in the water at the beach.

But in the end, I stopped telling anyone, not knowing how to explain fully, what this man was doing to me. I started to feel like I was living with a dark secret deep within myself. It was as though there was a cloud over my heart, due to the guilt and shame I felt. I even wondered if it was somehow my fault and that maybe I deserved to be treated this way. So, I learnt it was best to just put up with the abuse.

My way of coping was to lose myself in an imaginary world as I played on our farm amongst the animals. There was a large tree between our farmhouse and the dairy that my sisters called 'the magic tree', and it almost always made me feel happy to visit there. I often sat under it, imagining that I was someone else. A happy child with no problems in her life.

Despite all of this, I think I was a fairly well-behaved little girl. I would occasionally get the strap, or a hard crack around the behind, which I more than likely deserved. There is an old saying, 'Spare the rod and spoil the child'. I kept myself busy by playing lots of sport and had many friends, which helped me to blot out the memories of the abuse.

## Chapter Two

## Lynne and Me

### —1957-1964—

When I was approximately five years old, something very strange began to occur in my bedroom at night. In the early hours of the morning, two 'ladies' would visit, sit on the end of my bed and talk to me. They were old and quite ugly and spoke of things I no longer remember. I would wake from a deep sleep, sensing their presence as soon as they entered my room.

It was a little scary, but at the same time, exciting. I wanted the world to know. I used to call my mum with the hope that she also could have the opportunity to meet them. Poor Mum would come rushing down the hallway still half asleep, expecting that I was suffering from earache, (which I regularly did as a child), or that I was having another of what she referred to as 'nightmares about the unusual ladies'. As soon as she turned on the light and the darkness left my room, my 'friends' also disappeared. I was deeply disappointed, as I wanted her to witness them and believe that they were real.

I described my 'night friends' to her excitedly, but Mum kept telling me I was just imagining things. It seemed to me that she always thought I was imagining everything. But I continued to call her, hoping that she would witness herself, that these friends were not imaginary at all; and neither was I 'just dreaming'. Mum eventually became tired of being awakened each night by my urgent cries for her to 'come and see' and warned me sternly not to wake her unless it was a matter of extreme urgency. My father and mother needed to rise early to attend to farm duties, so both longed for sleep without interruption, if at all possible. However, my 'friends' kept coming to me until I was seven years old, then all of a sudden their visitations ceased.

Then something equally as strange started happening. At the front of our farmhouse, there was a set of old wooden stairs leading up onto the veranda. One day while sitting on the top step, a group of 'people' suddenly appeared, and began talking with me. This became a regular occurrence in broad daylight, whenever I sat on those stairs. These people were surrounded by light. There were usually fifteen to twenty of them at a time, and they made me laugh and laugh with some of the things they said to me. Once again, I cannot remember our conversations, but they brought joy to my life. I thought *everyone* could see them, so I was not at all embarrassed about having long conversations with them, even when my family or relatives were present.

I was certain our dog and cats could see them also as they sat on the steps beside me whenever these gatherings took place. I was so engrossed with my visitors that I was usually oblivious to anything else going on around me at the time. That was, until one day as I sat chatting away with my 'friends', I heard laughter coming from behind me, and realised it was one of my older siblings. She told me that I was a spastic. At the time, I really had no idea why she would call me that. On another occasion, I overheard my mum explaining to our cousins who were visiting the farm from Melbourne for Christmas, 'Don't take any notice of her. She has such a good imagination and a lot of imaginary friends you know'. One of my cousins still remembers Mum telling her this. I do not know who or what these 'people' were, but to me, they were very real. But as time went on, I began to take notice of what my mum was saying to people regarding my imagination, and by the age of eight, I did my upmost to avoid my 'friends', until eventually they no longer came to visit.

I was a reasonably happy child despite the fact that I was a little different. One thing that made me sad, though, and began to have a significant impact on my life, was the continuing sexual abuse that happened at most of the social events we attended as a family. These particular outings only occurred four to six times a year maximum, but despite the infrequency of the abuse, I found it difficult to keep what was happening, to myself. I began self-harming one day following a particularly cruel attack on my young body by this man. I was nine years old at the time. I felt ashamed, frustrated and angry about what had just taken place, and ripped and tore at my skin with my fingernails, until I bled. I was angry with him for hurting me and for deceiving everyone I loved into believing he was innocent.

To begin with, I only scratched myself in areas that were hidden from sight. Usually my tummy or the tops of my legs. Once though, I was so angry after one such incident that I tore at my arms until they were so scratched and bleeding, that my parents noticed. They took me immediately to our family doctor, whom at first was baffled as to the cause. My mum explained to him that I would often lie on the grass in our front yard. I used to lie there and gaze at the clouds and make up stories to correspond to the shape of each one. So, with that information, the doctor immediately diagnosed me as having an allergy to grass seed. I remember loving the attention I received as my mum applied the ointment the doctor had prescribed to my arms, and then wrapped them in bandages. It was almost like she was recognising my pain and shame from the abuse and was showing me compassion to make up for her non-belief of what this man was actually doing. Obviously, this was all in my mind, but I soaked up the love I felt she was showing me anyway.

My years at Primary School made up for the heaviness in my heart. I met a friend named Lynne in Kindergarten, and we are still friends to this day. She is so special to me. She had a lot of heaviness in her young heart also. Her dad passed away when she was not more than five years old. My mum invited her to the farm to stay with us for a few weeks after this sad event. We had so much fun – roaming the hills, exploring along the creek bank, making cubby houses up in the trees and swinging on a rope swing we made. It seemed to help to take her mind off things for a while, and it certainly helped me with the confusion and emotional pain I was feeling. We were two little broken girls, together.

As we grew older, Lynne and I had many sleepovers. Sometimes I would go to her place in town for the night. I loved sleeping over at hers, mainly because we could do 'townie' things such as visit the local café and drink milk shakes and eat cream buns. She loved to come to the farm and do all the adventurous things we had to do out there. She was totally unafraid of spiders and snakes and other 'creepy crawlies', which frightened some of my other town friends so much, that when they slept the night at our house, Mum, quite often, had to phone their parents, sometimes in the middle of the night, to come and fetch them. Lynne and I quite often visited other children with whom we were friends, who lived further along the country road from our farm.

One afternoon we were playing at a farm approximately two kilometres from our house with another girlfriend of ours. We decided to do a 'dare' that night. Lynne and I were to return to my house, wait until dark, then walk back again to the other friend's home. To prove that we had actually done this, we were to place a note in our other friend's mailbox.

When we came back home that day, I ran the idea of our dare past my mother, and she agreed to allow us to carry out our plan. So, we wrote the note and set out, at around seven pm. It was a beautiful moonlit night, and on the way, just out of the blue, Lynne let out the biggest burp I had ever heard. We laughed so much we almost fell down. I asked her how she did it, and she told me that it was best to lie down, suck a burp up to your throat, leave it there, suck another and another and another, until you physically felt ill. Then, in her words, 'you let it rip'. I was impressed.

So, we lay down in the middle of the country road, side by side, and I learnt under Lynne's skilful instructions, how to do these monster burps. Before too long, I was almost as proficient as Lynne was at this gross skill.

We wandered on towards our friend's house, laughing and burping along the way, despite the fact that we were both beginning to feel quite sick in the tummy. As we approached her farmhouse, we heard our friend singing, as her mother accompanied her on the piano. She was gifted with a beautiful soprano voice. Although Lynne and I realised that she was an exceptionally good singer, we did not appreciate the fact. She and I were more interested in The Beatles, the famous pop group from England. Despite that, we got a little carried away and completely by-passed the mailbox where we were supposed to place our note, distracted by the music as it permeated the night. As we climbed the front stairs, we did not even think about letting my friend and her mum know we were there. We simply were going to sit a while, listen to the music, place our note in the mailbox, and be on our way.

We quietly climbed the front stairs of the old farmhouse. As we approached the top step, we could clearly see our friend and her mum, sitting side by side on a piano stool with their backs to us at the end of the long hallway. The top step made a loud creaking noise as Lynne and I both sat down at the same time. Spooked by this sound, our soprano friend's mother stopped playing the piano, her hands frozen temporarily in mid-air. Our friend ceased singing. Her mother then leapt to her feet, grabbed a flashlight, turned off every light in that house, and via torchlight proceeded with caution down the hallway, all the while clinging tightly to her daughter's hand. At the same time all this was taking place Lynne and I, not wishing to be discovered for fear of being in deep trouble for frightening them, quickly scurried through a set of French doors on the side of the veranda into the front bedroom, where we crawled under the single bed.

The only problem was that under the bed was a full chamber pot. I almost put my head in it in my haste to hide. We got the nervous giggles but soon contained ourselves as the light from the torch came closer and closer until mother and daughter entered the bedroom. Lynne and I could see the mother's slippered feet approaching the bed. She picked up the corner of the chenille single bedspread and began to reprimand her daughter saying, 'What is this pile of dirty clothes doing under your bed'? Of course, we were the 'dirty clothes' to whom she was referring. We were discovered and scolded for frightening my friend's mum and her and causing them to think they had a prowler. We sincerely apologised, and realising the folly of our ways, hand-delivered the dare note to our soprano friend and proceeded to walk further down the road.

Folks in this area, as well as surrounding areas of Mullumbimby, had been a little nervous lately, as there had been quite a few suspicious house fires supposedly started by a firebug. These fires were always started in deserted, derelict, about-to-be-condemned type houses. As Lynne and I continued to walk further down the country road, we decided to practice our 'burping' skills again and became so engrossed in this activity that we did not realise we were across the road from yet another farmhouse. Our burps echoed loudly in the night. Lynne made me laugh. She brightened my life so much. But all of a sudden, the night seemed to get darker, and we realised all the lights in the house had been turned off. We quickly lay down in the long grass beside the road, as the farmer released his two savage cattle dogs through the front gate. We lay motionless, hugging each other. The sound of the approaching dogs terrified us, as they sniffed their way through the long grass. Finally, the farmer whistled for them to come home. Grateful that we had not been detected, we lay still until the lights in the farmhouse came back on and then tentatively began the walk back to my place.

When we were almost home, a police car rounded the bend and pulled up beside us. It seemed that the farmer at the second residence had called the police, reporting 'loud noises' erupting from somewhere quite near his house. We hung our heads in shame as we admitted that it had been us, 'just practising our burping'. The policeman told Lynne and me off well and properly for disturbing the farmer, who thought it may have been the notorious firebug, attempting to set fire to an old country dance hall situated quite near to his farm. The police officer ordered Lynne and me to get into the police car, and as he dropped us off at my front gate, he told us sternly that we were to tell our parents what we had done. Even though we were terrified of the police back in those days, I do not remember relaying that message to my parents. And as far as I know, our soprano friend's mum did not alert my parents to the incident either.

When I was eleven years old, our family and I attended the yearly Sunday School picnic at the beach. Even though I felt excited at the prospect of spending the day with friends, I dreaded the thought of possibly being assaulted yet again. Just lately, though, I had noticed at other social events, some of the parents of children much younger than I were beginning to suspect that this man was up to no good and made sure they were close to their children at all times. He had started to stalk and follow other young girls, as well.

My friends and I raced each other to see who could be first into the water. It was not long before the sexual offender slinked across the hot white sand and entered the river, remaining in the shallows for a while, observing the children. This was his normal pattern of behaviour. He always stood back and watched, like a wild animal sizing up its prey. He approached my friends and me and began a game of 'catch' with us. Once again, I was his target, and he caught me and began touching me inappropriately. I was a lot stronger than the last time he had attempted this and struggled to get away from him. He would not release me, so I began yelling at him, and then I struck him across the face. The next thing I remember was my dad pulling me from the water, reprimanding me once again for being disrespectful to my elders. Here it was, happening again in the same way as every other time. I was sent to the hot car for the day, while all the other children enjoyed playing together in the water and eating watermelon and other tasty treats.

On this particular day, I felt more anger towards this man than I ever had previously. I lay down along the bench seat of the FJ Holden and cried in sheer frustration. This was so unfair. How dare this man continue to do this to me? As my salty tears stung my eyes, a shadow fell across my face and I tilted my head backwards only to see the predator with his head through the car window, staring down the front of my one-piece swimsuit. 'Developing nicely,' he muttered.

With that, I sat bolt upright, faced that man and informed him that if ever he touched me again, I would report him to the police. I told him that even though no one else believed me, the police would. Thanks be to God; he never came near me again.

About one year prior to my mother's passing, she asked me why I had made such a mess of my life. Without making excuses for any of the bad decisions I had made, I reminded her of this man and told her of what he had done to me. She seemed shocked and explained that whilst my father and she had suspected something due to the way

I reacted each time he came near me, they did not realise the extent of the abuse. She was saddened by this and so was I. But at the same time, I understood that in those days, most people did not talk about anything sexual. Unfortunately, this meant most offenders were not punished, because the offences were to be kept a secret. Sadly, without any form of justice, victims of sexual abuse from this period of time (and before) carry their scars for life.

## Chapter Three

## Close Call in our Farm Creek

## —1964—

One day, another friend from a neighbouring farm came to visit, and we headed off down to the creek bank to play. She showed me a packet of Viscount cigarettes she had hidden in her backpack, and we decided to experiment and find out what it was like to smoke. We almost choked to death, but we persisted anyway, feeling very grown up and so 'cool', despite the fact that we both turned a pale shade of purple. Cigarette smoking was promoted and encouraged back then, and advertisements on television and in magazines conveyed that if you smoked, you were very sophisticated and somehow even more attractive. Unfortunately, I became addicted to nicotine at a young age and continued to smoke for many years.

Sometimes I felt so tormented by my mind that I gouged chunks of skin from my body until I bled, still making sure the injuries I inflicted on myself were not anywhere that they would be seen. Strangely enough I felt better whilst in the process of self-harming, as it was like I was punishing myself for being ugly and bad. Whilst I had once loved to go to church with my family, and even though the sexual offender had ceased pursuing me, I dreaded it now as he still attended. He made no secret of the fact that he was still interested in looking at my young, developing body. I thought I would throw up as he ogled me quite openly. One day, his daughter approached me and asked if her dad had been touching me. At first, I was shocked that she would ask such a thing and denied that he had. But when she revealed to me that her father had raped her once and that no one believed her, I told her the truth. As sick as this may sound, I felt a little better that she had confided in me. It was almost as though I had an ally. And that someone actually believed me. I felt incredibly sad for her though.

When I was approximately twelve years old, my parents decided to enrol my older sister and me in swimming lessons offered by the surf lifesaving club at a beach not far from our farm. My sister, already a reasonably competent swimmer, was enrolled in a Bronze Medallion class which taught her to perform basic water rescues and to provide Cardiopulmonary Resuscitation (CPR). I was in a beginner's class and, as I recall, to be deemed competent, we had to jump into the water from a rowing boat, tread water for a certain amount of time, then swim approximately twenty-two yards to shore. My lessons took place in shallow water at the river's edge to begin with, and then once everyone in the class was confident, we were taken by boat to the middle of the river. My sister passed her Bronze Medallion one week prior to my final assessment.

On the day of my test, it was drizzling with rain. The river appeared rather ominous and a bit scary, reflecting an eerie green/grey colour due to the dullness of the day. I felt sick to my stomach with nerves at the thought of jumping out of the boat into the murky depths. But I wanted this certificate so badly that eventually, when it was my turn to be assessed, I plucked up the courage, took the plunge and passed all of the required competencies. I felt proud of my achievement when the instructor handed me my certificate. As my dad drove me back to the farm, I was filled with excitement at the thought of showing the rest of the family my award. As soon as we arrived, I hurriedly left the car and ran into the kitchen where my mum was, busily baking cookies and cakes for the coming week. This was her Saturday routine after she had finished milking cows in the morning, cleaning the farmhouse and doing the washing, using a washboard, copper and hand wringer to complete the job.

I quickly showed my certificate to my mother and then asked her where my older sister was, as I could barely wait another minute to share my great news with her. Mum informed me that she was swimming in our farm creek with three of her friends, and that I was best to not go annoying them. However, my mother's warning fell on deaf ears. I took off at a pace, running excitedly to the creek without another thought of the advice I had just received. I heard my sister and her friends' laughter before I located them. Down the creek bank I dashed, waving my award in the breeze. I totally ignored the horrified look on my sister's face as she turned when she heard my excited greeting. There were four girls including her, rowing along happily in an old milk vat up and down the creek. Happily, that was, until I arrived.

'What are you doing here', my sister shouted at me angrily.

'I passed my swim test', I stated proudly.

'How far did you swim?' she enquired with disbelief in her voice.

'Twenty-two yards' I replied.

'Well, prove it' she snapped at me.

With that, I checked the distance from where I was standing on the bank to where they were in the vat, guessing it was approximately the same as I had swum in order to pass my test. Maybe not even as far? I could do this easily, and then maybe my sister would invite me to stay and have fun with them. I secured my certificate under a rock before plunging confidently into the water and swimming towards where the girls were in that old milk vat. As I swam, my sister and her friends paddled further away from me, laughing as they went, not realising the danger they were placing me in. Before long, I began to tire. And shortly after that, I was fighting for my life as I struggled to keep my head above the water. I soon ran out of breath and began to sink below the surface. I was terrified, to say the least, but, as I began to lose consciousness, three things happened that I would never forget.

Firstly, as I began to sink down through the partly murky creek water, I could see the fingers of my sister and her friends, as they frantically dived, trying to save me. The next thing I remember, I began to feel peace and hoped my mum and dad would not worry too much about not having me around anymore. Then, as a state of unconsciousness enveloped me, I heard the most amazing music that I have ever heard in my life. It was not of this world. It was from Heaven. When I try to explain this to others, they often ask me to describe it. I cannot describe something from the spirit realm. All I can say is that it was heavenly. Then I slipped into unconsciousness. The next thing I remember is becoming aware that I was no longer in the water and that I was lying on the creek bank. My sister was in the process of administering CPR, and she and the girls were all crying. She had saved my life, even though I must have been the biggest pest to her back then.

Approximately twenty-eight years later, just prior to her death, my mum asked me about this incident. She knew that something really bad had happened to me in the farm creek and she wanted me to tell her about it. I did not wish to reveal anything to her, but she pleaded with me. She told me it would not worry her, but she just needed to know. So, I told her. She seemed more peaceful after hearing this, and not long afterwards, she passed away.

## Chapter Four

# My First Place of Employment

### —1964-1967—

When my closest friend Lynne and I were eleven and a half years old, we began high school together. I struggled academically in primary, so I found it even more difficult to understand most of my high school subjects. Even though I tried hard, it seemed as though my brain could not process the information. Strangely enough, I excelled in Music, English, Home Economics and loved sports. As time went on, I tried even harder to please everybody, often engaging in behaviour which went against my own values. My peers elected me class captain a couple of years running. I guess this was because I was everybody's friend and would never 'dob' on anyone in the class for doing the wrong thing, should the teacher leave me in charge for any length of time.

Meanwhile, a new family moved into our farming community, and I began dating one of the boys, who was a couple of years older than me. His family was very musical, and the children formed their own rock and roll band. It wasn't long before word of their wonderful musical capabilities spread, and they were in great demand for dances and parties. My boyfriend and I only saw each other on the cream lorry on the way to and from school and occasionally, at one of the popular swimming holes. This was where lots of the farm kids hung out together on weekends. He quite often invited me to accompany him to local dances where his band was performing, but my parents refused to allow me to attend despite my pleas. Understandably so, I was only thirteen or fourteen years old at the time.

But as kids do, I didn't give up. One day I asked my parents, yet again, if I could accompany my boyfriend to a dance. After discussing my request with Dad, I was shocked when Mum said they had decided I would be allowed to go to the dance. As it turned out, there was a movie screening that my parents wished to see. It just so happened to be at the theatre in the same town where the band was scheduled to play. I was very surprised that my parents were allowing me to attend the dance by myself. Even though this particular place was a popular tourist destination, it was also known to be a haven for drugs and other undesirable activities. My mum and dad often remarked that 'no good ever came out of that town'. My parents stipulated that they would drive me to the dance, attend the movie with my younger brother, then pick me up at a given time, at a set location. I was so excited, I could barely sleep at night, as I counted down the days prior to this outing.

My parents dropped me off outside the dance, giving me strict instructions as to what time they would come back for me and where I was to wait for them. I was so grateful that they trusted me and was not about to abuse that privilege by arriving late for 'pick up', or doing anything else for that matter, that would cause them disappointment. As I approached the dance hall, I noticed that the doors had not yet opened. I peeked through a side window and could see my boyfriend and his brothers setting up their instruments. Realising I was a little early, I felt I had no choice but to wait outside until the dance started.

Even though I was very excited, I felt nervous as I stood by myself in the dimly lit street. I was too timid to ask for anything for myself back then and would never have even dreamed about knocking on the door and asking my boyfriend if I could come inside and wait. In hindsight, if I had done so, he would have wanted me to be with him, out of any potential danger. But I didn't want to bother anyone.

After five minutes or so, a man approached me, introduced himself and struck up a conversation. I realised he was a little older than me, but he seemed like a nice bloke and appeared to be concerned that I was waiting outside in the dark alone. He enquired as to why I was there, so I explained to him how my parents had dropped me off so I could meet up with my boyfriend who was a drummer in the band. I had arrived a little early and was simply waiting for the doors to open and the dance to begin. He asked if I would like a milkshake, 'just to fill in time', and I accepted. After all, it seemed a better option at the time than waiting alone in the dark. He seemed nice enough, and the fact that he was older than I was, made me feel almost as though he was acting like an older brother, protecting me in a sense. He had a car, so he suggested that we drive to the milk bar.

But instead of driving to the café down the road from the dance, (and beside the movie theatre where my parents and little brother were,) the man drove to a remote part of the town. I was terrified when I realised that I had trusted a monster. When he pulled into bushland and stopped the car, I attempted to escape, but did not even get to open the car door. The man held me down roughly and raped me, then drove back to the front of the dance hall, pushed me from the car before driving away at speed. I crossed the street and hid in the dark near the designated meeting place and waited for my parents to pick me up. I felt mixed emotions of deep sadness, fear, shame and regret as I recalled the events of the evening. When I saw our car approaching, I stepped out of the darkness into the headlights of Dad's car, my beautiful pink and white satin dress Mum had sewn for me, torn and covered in blood. It was evident I had been assaulted, so Mum began firing questions at me as to what had happened. I told my parents exactly what had taken place.

My dad began to drive towards the police station, but Mum suggested instead that we go straight home. There was nothing more said. The silence was deafening. What did they think of me? I had done wrong yet again. What a disappointment I must have been to them. But I could not understand why I had been sexually assaulted. My mind was flooded with thoughts of my unworthiness. It seemed like whenever a predator took advantage of my innocence, the whole thing was simply swept under the carpet. It was obvious that Mum and Dad did not know how to deal with what had taken place. And more to the point, back in those days, you did your best not to bring shame upon the family at any cost. And the victim in situations such as this was often considered to be almost as guilty as the perpetrator. There was also the fear that if word somehow got around, the story may be published in the local paper, and that could bring ill repute upon the family name.

A short time after this horrific offence was committed against me, I was visiting a friend who had invited me to sleep over at her house. I had not known this girl long and when I arrived at her home, I realised that her mum and dad were not there. When I asked my friend about this, she told me that her parents had gone away for the weekend, leaving her older brother and her at home alone. A short time later, my friend's brother called us both into his bedroom, but my friend did not stay, instead making an excuse and leaving the room. Her brother locked the door, dragged me forcefully to his bed and raped me. When he finally let me go, I asked my friend if I could use her phone to call my parents to come and pick me up. She did not even ask me why I had changed my mind about staying the night. My parents thought it was rather odd that they had only just dropped me off for a sleepover, yet now I was asking to be picked up. I made some excuse about not feeling well and after this horrible incident, this girl and I never spoke to one another again. It was as though she knew what her brother had done to me, and maybe had even been aware of his intentions, prior to my visit.

Our family faithfully attended church each Sunday, and I began to help out as an assistant teacher in Sunday school. I feared God back then, but it was not with a reverent, healthy fear. My thoughts about Him were that He was a very angry God who watched me from heaven, just waiting for me to do something wrong. I figured I had done so much wrong that there was no turning back. So, I tried to block thoughts of Him from my mind through the week, dealing with my feelings of guilt and shame on Sunday mornings in church. I never realised that God was the total opposite of what I thought, and that He loved me, despite my sinful nature.

My friend Lynne and I continued to get up to all sorts of mischief. I used to think that our teenage years were absolutely the most fun and exciting, (though dangerous,) years of my life. Often, we would hitch-hike to dances, pubs or music venues, telling our parents we were sleeping over at each other's houses. Lynne helped me to temporarily forget about the sexual abuse from my childhood and the two more recent assaults that had occurred. Our times together were usually filled with laughter. We both sat for the Intermediate Certificate when we were fourteen years old, and I just barely passed. My parents could see I was struggling, so they told me if I could find a job, they would consent to me leaving school. A new hairdressing salon had just opened in town and the owner was advertising for a first-year apprentice. I applied and my application was successful.

At first, I was excited to be out of school and earning a wage which at the time for a first-year apprentice hairdresser, was eleven dollars and sixty-eight cents per week. I felt very grown up and had money left over even after paying board to my parents. But the highlight of my job was that I worked with the most beautiful lady I had ever seen. She was my senior and the manageress of the salon. My dad drove me to and from work. This was such a sacrifice on his behalf as he was busy on the farm, milking cows, ploughing fields in preparation to plant feed for the cattle, as well as the normal maintenance of fences and other farm duties.

The owner of the hairdressing salon came to check on my senior and me twice per week. She owned another salon approximately forty-five-minute drive from our town. Everything seemed to be running smoothly to start with, but then I began to notice our boss often inviting my senior for 'a talk', in the back room with the door closed. I could not help but think that for one reason or another, the senior was being reprimanded. This surprised me, because since opening this new salon with the senior hairdresser managing it, we were so booked that people often had to wait weeks for an appointment. Word had definitely spread throughout our small town about the creative cutting and styling techniques of this talented hairdresser. There was one other hair salon in our town, and its business suffered due to the fact that most of their clients began seeking our services.

I also noticed the manageress' once happy demeanour, gradually changing. Her face was often etched with worry and sadness, as though she carried the weight of the world on her shoulders. Being at least ten years younger, I did not really know how to approach her and ask if I could help. One day she broke down and warned me to be very careful of our superior. She told me that our boss drank very heavily after work each night, which caused her a hangover. This was the reason she was so unreasonable and angry in more ways than one. I was very grateful that I had been warned, but this did not dampen my passion to learn all I could about hairdressing. In no time at all, I was cutting, tinting, perming and performing all of the tasks required of a fully qualified hairdresser.

I loved my job, even though the owner of the salon was beginning to give me a hard time, as well. One day, she accused me of stealing from her when the banking was five cents short. She took me to the back room and slapped me across the face with such force that I fell to the floor. On another occasion, I was tinting a client's hair as my boss looked on. A small drop of tint managed to escape my tinting brush, and as I bent to wipe it from the floor, she grabbed me by the hair and pulled me to an upright position, cracking my head against the side of the ceramic washbasin with such force that I saw stars before my eyes. She then took me by the arm and led me forcefully to the back room where she slapped my face for embarrassing her in front of the lady whose hair I was colouring. Consequently, our regular clients began to book their appointments on the days my boss wasn't present.

Despite all of this and due to my senior's passion to teach me all she knew, my clientele began to grow at a rapid pace. I entered into the second year of my apprenticeship, and my pay increased to thirteen dollars per week. I told my parents about what was happening at work and how I was being mistreated by my boss, but they told me to 'stick at it', as I was lucky to have a job. It seemed I had no option, so I decided to just put up with things as they were.

One day just prior to closing time, either the senior or I accidentally knocked a decorative crystal bell off the reception desk. We literally froze with fear as we surveyed the shattered glass on the floor. Once we had composed ourselves, we locked the doors of the salon and ran to the jewellery shop around the corner. We found an exact replica of the bell, and I remember clearly that my half of the purchase price was my entire week's wage. On arrival back at the salon, we carefully swept all evidence of our mishap into the bin and placed the new identical bell carefully onto the counter. Despite the price we paid, we both agreed that it was well worth it. Anything instead of bearing the brunt of our boss's angry tirade, supposing she somehow found out about our accidental mishap.

The very next day, I arrived for work and walked straight into a war zone. The owner of the salon, face contorted and red with fury, was screaming at top note, obviously in the process of sacking my senior on the grounds of dishonesty. She had arrived early and discovered the pieces of crystal in the trash, and because we had tried to cover our 'terrible crime,' my beautiful senior was being dismissed. This was the last straw for me. I was so filled with fear at the boss's unjustified anger, that I turned and ran to the safety of the grocery shop next door. I hovered at the ends of aisles, pretending to be looking for something, until I thought the coast was clear.

Taking off like a scared rabbit, I headed to Lynne's auntie's house. My parents were away at the time and I was staying there until they returned. I was still shaking when I finally arrived, and through my tears I poured out my story to her, all the while thinking she was going to make me return to that salon, simply because she was responsible for me. To my surprise, Auntie told me not to go back there ever, because as far as she was concerned, I had been the victim of abuse. She promised to take full responsibility for her decision and explain her reasoning to my parents. She kept her word, and on my parents' return, she explained to them what had taken place and her thoughts on the mistreatment I had suffered. After hearing this, Mum and Dad both agreed that this job was not in my best interest.

My parents purchased a beautiful block of land at Brunswick Heads, bordered by the surf beach immediately across the road at the front, and a river at the back. A traffic bridge and separate foot bridge connected our street to the small village. My folks planned to build their retirement home on the block when they sold the farm. My dad suggested that he rent a space for a hair salon in the village, placing my senior as manageress in order for me to finish my apprenticeship. However, I was so young at the time and the treatment my senior and I had endured at the hands of our cruel boss left me with no desire to return to hairdressing ever again. Not long after this, the farm sold, and my parents, my younger brother and I moved to the beach. My older sisters had since, left home.

## Chapter Five

## Shattered Dreams

### —1967-1969—

My father arranged for the garage at the back of our beach block to be converted into a liveable shed as a temporary dwelling for us. Work began on our home soon after we moved. Dad enjoyed helping the labourers, as he had been in the farming industry for most of his working life and was finding it difficult to relax since he had retired. My younger brother and I loved living at the beach. He and I spent most of our spare time fishing, swimming, and surfing with our friends on weekends. Mum and I delighted in eating fresh oysters directly from the rocks at the back of our block, and life began to feel as though it could not possibly get any better.

My friend Lynne and I caught a bus three days per week to a nearby Business College to attend a shorthand/typing course. We played sports on Saturdays and usually had 'sleep-overs' at each other's place on Saturday nights. We continued our dangerous habit of hitchhiking if ever we wished to travel any distance away from our homes. It was a practise you would never dream of now, but still risky even back then.

Publicans and staff at hotels we ventured into allowed us to drink alcohol with no questions asked. We were only fifteen or sixteen at the time. Alcohol was served to minors in most hotels back then, even though the bar-staff were well aware that they were serving kids. The legal age to drink in New South Wales was twenty-one. Sometimes the police would raid the pub, but somehow the publican would get wind of the impending raid and usher the underage drinkers into the toilets, where we stayed until the coast was clear. Lynne and I only ever consumed two small glasses of sweet sherry each. That was all we could afford, and it was enough to make us feel a little tipsy.

One night we were travelling in a Holden with some of our mates, five abreast across the bench seat in the front, with no seat belts in those days. We were not going at a great speed, but the driver took a corner a little too fast, the passenger door flew open and because I was closest to that door, I fell out of the car onto the road. As a result, I was left with a bad gravel rash and hurting like crazy. Instead of crying like I wanted to, I swallowed my pride and laughed as my mates hoisted me back into the car. We did a lot of other extremely dangerous and stupid things. We thought we were just having harmless fun, but fun can lead to disaster, heartache and pain.

One Saturday afternoon after we finished playing a game of netball, Lynne and I were approached by two boys. They introduced themselves to us and struck up a conversation. We talked for a while, then just prior to us going our separate ways, they invited us to meet with them later that evening. We accepted their request, met them in a local park that night and before long we were double dating. (Lynne ended up marrying one of these young men a few years later.) Unbeknown to me at the time, I ended up with the 'bad boy'. He was rough and tough and quite a few years older than I was. It was not long before one thing led to another and we slept together. I felt guilty about what we had done and broke off the relationship. Not long after, I met one of the bricklayers who was helping to build our home and began dating him. We had a lot in common and enjoyed each other's company immensely. But I started to notice that I felt very nauseous from the smell of certain foods, and I began to spend a lot of time sick in our temporary outhouse.

One weekend when Lynne slept over, I was throwing up after dinner as usual. She asked me the obvious question; 'Do you think you may be pregnant?' I had not even thought of this until then. It suddenly dawned on me that was probably the reason why I was so ill. I thought at the time, that you had to have intercourse several times before you could become pregnant. Whilst at school I had learnt a lot from listening to older girls discussing sex in the toilet block in the lunch break. But I did not necessarily learn the right things.

Mum used to put a mattress under the dining table in our temporary dwelling for Lynne and me to sleep on whenever she stayed over. That night, I lay beside her on the mattress and sobbed quietly as I poured out my heart to her. She was a good friend and a great comfort to me, but I knew in my heart that for the next six months or so, I would be more than likely doing life alone. How was I to tell my parents? Oh, what shame I was bringing to our family. Also, I had just started dating who I thought was the most amazing boy. He would surely want nothing to do with me now, especially since I was carrying someone else's baby.

The very next afternoon, I invited my mum to go fishing with me. This definitely was not her favourite pastime, but she reluctantly accepted my invitation. I wanted to have her to myself without Dad, so I could break the news to her. We sat side by side about halfway down the break-wall in front of our house, our fishing lines moving to and fro in the waves. There were no fish. Not even a nibble. Mum wanted to leave after about ten minutes, but I feigned massive bites and this huge phantom fish that I just kept missing and was not about to give up on. I would start to steer our conversation in such a way that I could tell her about me being pregnant, then fear would take over and cause me to become totally tongue-tied. I was absolutely terrified about what her reaction would be. I was shaking and felt sick to the pit of my stomach. It began to get dark and I could fake the phantom fish no longer. My mum was anxious to get home and begin dinner. So, I just spat it out. 'I'm pregnant'. I thought she was going to fall off the rocks into the water as the realisation of what I had just told her sunk in. She was so terribly upset, and I do not blame her for this.

We walked home together without speaking another word to each other. I felt ashamed of myself and I wanted her to yell at me and get it over and done with. But she did not. When we arrived home, I went straight to my room. It was not long before my mum appeared in the doorway as I lay on my bed and broke the news to me. My father and she had decided that I had to leave. There was no other choice. I had to go 'somewhere', and soon. Where, she did not say. Just away from the family and the town where we lived, so that I would not bring shame upon them. I knew this would happen, as that was just how it was back then. I had heard rumours of other girls who had become pregnant suddenly disappearing and returning months later. She insisted I tell the 'nice boy' I was dating, that I was pregnant, and that was not negotiable. I found it extremely hard to tell my boyfriend, but he reacted to my news in the most surprising way. He told me he loved me and wanted to continue a relationship with me.

Over the next few days, my mind became my worst enemy. My thoughts were consumed with how bad I was, and I wished for this all to just be a nightmare that I would soon awaken from. The shame I thought I had brought upon my family lately seemed to be ongoing. I began to think of ways to end it all by taking my life and decided to drown myself.

After dinner, a few days later, I pretended I needed to go to the outhouse, but instead of returning to the shed, I kept on walking until

I reached the break-wall. I sat and planned what measures to take in order to drown as I watched wave after massive wave pound onto the rocks below. I cannot remember the exact details of what happened that night, but I obviously chickened out as I imagined myself becoming mincemeat against the rocks if I carried out my plan. I also recalled the sheer terror I had felt in the farm creek the day my sister and her friends miraculously saved me from drowning.

With these thoughts swirling through my mind, I left the turbulence of the waves and walked back to the road, past our block to the surf club. I lay down on a bench seat in one of the rooms, in a state of sheer exhaustion. The next thing I knew, I was being woken by a police officer. He informed me my mum had reported me missing. I do not recall the conversation that took place between the officer and myself, but I do remember him being truly kind and compassionate as I explained my situation to him. We spoke further and then he drove me back to our temporary home. My parents' faces were etched with sadness when I faced them again that night, and they explained to me that I would have to leave the very next day. I understood. I knew there was a penalty for what I had done. I did not think badly of them and still do not to this day. That was the way it was back then. 'Nice girls' did not get pregnant. But it does not mean I was not scared half to death.

The next morning, I packed my bag and just prior to me walking out the door, Mum handed me a five-dollar note. I trudged up the lane behind our shed, head bowed in shame. There was a travel agent in our small community, so I decided to enquire there, so as to give me some idea of my destination, of which at this point, I had no clue.

'Where to?' said the man gruffly from behind the counter.

'I don't know. How far will five dollars take me?' I replied, with tears filling my eyes.

'There is a bus to Brisbane that will cost you that amount, and it is departing within the hour,' he informed me.

I handed over all the money I had in the world in exchange for the fare. But now that I had discovered my destination, I felt even more frightened. I was a country girl. Maybe once or twice Dad had driven us to the outskirts of this city where a 'Pilot' would meet with us at a pre-arranged point. He would then drive our car into the city in order for my family to carry out whatever business they needed to do. I remembered the 'busyness', tall buildings and noise as buses and trams wended their way along grey, dismal streets packed with people; all in a hurry going 'somewhere'.

I walked outside and sat on a bench seat, waiting for the bus to come. I could see the back of our shed from there, and as I sat, I willed for my father to come and pick me up and tell me everything was going to be all right. That he and my mum had decided to look after me. This was my wish, but it did not happen. A short time later, a Greyhound bus pulled to a halt right in front of me. The trip to Brisbane was one fraught with anxiety. Where would I go when I arrived? I did not know anyone in this city. What would happen to my baby and me? As I began to think of the tiny baby growing within me, I suddenly did not feel quite so alone. It was actually comforting to think that I was not going through this by myself. Soon there would be two of us, and I would protect this little one at any cost.

When we arrived in Brisbane, passengers disembarked here and there along the way, till only the driver and I remained on board the bus. He then drove to the depot and I knew I had reached my destination and had to depart what had been a temporary safe haven for the past few hours. I thanked the driver and surveyed my new surroundings with trepidation. It was then that I noticed a church directly across the road from where I stood. Maybe I could ask for help right there. However, it was Saturday— surely, there would not be much hope of finding anyone in church until tomorrow. Then to my surprise, I realised that the front door was open. I lugged my heavy suitcase across the road, up the stairs and peered inside.

There was a man walking between the church pews, placing notices here and there at intervals along the rows. When I entered the church, he looked up and then approached me. He shook my hand and introduced himself as the pastor of the church. He asked if he could help me with anything. With that, I broke down and poured out my heart to him. Kindness and compassion oozed from this man, and I knew that I could trust him. He remained very calm as he listened to my story, then asked if I thought I could work for a while. I had mentioned to him that I had completed a shorthand/typing course quite recently. He told me he knew of a man who managed a vacuum cleaning company and was looking for someone with my qualifications. I agreed to 'give the job a go'.

The pastor made a phone call, then told me I was to report for work the following Monday. He found accommodation for me at a ladies' hostel and booked me into a home for unmarried mothers where I would go when I could no longer work. This kind man even helped me sort out which bus to catch to and from work each day. I was so grateful for all he had done for me and felt as though he had thrown me a lifeline and saved me from a sinking ship. He then drove me to the hostel and asked me to keep in touch and to let him know when I felt I could no longer work.

I felt so alone in that hostel. All the women were much older and none of them seemed to want to bother with me that much. The fact that I was so ill with morning sickness that lasted day and night also did not help. I spent most of the time at both the hostel and work in the bathroom being sick. After about four weeks it all became too much. I phoned the pastor and asked if he could take me to the home. I remained there for the next five months.

## Chapter Six

## The Home for Unmarried Mothers

### —1969-1970—

As I stood outside the 'home', I felt a surge of hope rise within me. The house itself appeared to be no different from the surrounding houses in the bayside suburb, and it looked almost welcoming. However, I did not notice the cold steel bars on the downstairs windows. I knocked tentatively at the door and a rather matronly looking lady greeted me. After I introduced myself, she beckoned for me to enter the dimly lit front entrance. As I followed her down a long corridor, I noticed girls of varying ages in the rooms we passed, each attending to some form of chore or another. They turned from their work and eyed me quizzically as we passed by. These girls appeared to be at different stages of their pregnancies, and I could not help but notice that each one of their faces was masked by sadness. I felt the hope I had initially experienced only minutes before suddenly drain from me

I was shown to my room and was shocked at how cold and stark it was. The atmosphere felt as though the previous occupant had left behind her very soul. There was a heaviness so oppressive I could barely stand it as I took in the space between the grey, forlorn, prison-like walls.

'Unpack' the matronly lady snapped at me.

I reluctantly began to remove my meagre belongings from my port, all the while under the eagle-like stare of this seemingly cold-hearted woman. Within an instant her demeanour changed from being stern to utter disgust, as I placed a very modest, black lingerie set that my 'very Presbyterian' mother had purchased for me, into the drawer of an ugly, old wardrobe in the corner of the room.

'Oh, so now I know why you got yourself into this disgusting condition,' she hissed. 'You can remove that along with most of the other items you have brought with you'. She began tugging at garments I had already hung on hangers in the wardrobe, hurling them at me, one by one along with the black underwear which had disgusted her so much. Her mission finally accomplished, she motioned to me with a tilt of her head, to follow her.

She set off down the long corridor, determination in each step, marching as though she had once been enlisted in the army. I almost had to run to keep up with her. At the end of the corridor we descended a set of stairs leading to the back yard. She then headed towards one corner of the yard to an incinerator, pulled my garments angrily from my grasp and hurled them through the front opening. To my shock and horror, she lit some scrunched-up newspaper, then carefully and purposefully set my precious clothing on fire. She then spun around and screeched, 'Now you can think about the despicable acts you have committed to get yourself into the shameful state you are in, as you watch these sinful clothes of yours burn. You are nothing but a little slut and your clothing and the fact that you are here in this home prove that you are. You and your type disgust me'.

The situation was unbearable. I tried to run from her, but she grabbed me by the arm and made me watch through my tears of hurt and shame as my belongings turned to ashes. I returned to the main house with her, where she found three or four of the ugliest maternity dresses I had ever seen and threw them at me. She ordered one of the other girls to show me around and delegate daily chores. I felt as though my very heart and soul had been shattered into a million pieces. I sighed with sheer relief as this cruel hearted woman turned to leave, seemingly happy with herself that she had bullied yet another young girl who had made the mistake of getting herself pregnant.

The rather nervous young girl familiarised me with the rules and regulations of the home, then placed a label with my name on it onto a spare pint of milk in the refrigerator. She told me I was to drink the entire bottle every day, as milk was good for my developing baby. She also explained that we were all to rest for one hour each afternoon, from one until two o'clock. She placed me on a rotating roster to carry out chores such as scrubbing floors (on hands and knees,) washing walls and windows, attending to laundry, ironing, sweeping, gardening etc. Except for our compulsory rest, we were not to be found 'lazing about'. If we finished our jobs, we did them again.

The young girl then informed me that church attendance was compulsory each Sunday, and there were also rules concerning this. She explained that, so as not to offend other church-goers by the condition we were in, we were to enter the church five minutes after the service had begun, sit in the back row, not make eye contact with any of the parishioners and depart five minutes prior to finishing time. I felt shame upon shame upon shame almost smothering me and dreaded the experience. The following Sunday I attempted to make excuses as to why I could not attend church to the supervisor on roster. However, she acted as though she was deaf. As we walked into church and filed into the back seats, some of the congregation turned to look at us, but the experience I had dreaded was nowhere nearly as bad as what I had imagined it would be. I actually enjoyed the outing, as we were stuck in the house working extremely hard for most of the week. And because we quietly left five minutes before everyone else, no one seemed to even notice our departure.

Christmas Day, 1969, seemed to come around very quickly. I remember sitting with my friend Wendy, discussing what was about to happen to us. We were the only ones in the home with no visitors that day. My relatives lived in New South Wales, and hers were in Western Australia. We held each other and cried, filled with fear for our babies and our future. What would become of our little ones and us? We were seventeen years old at the time. We spoke of the shame that was heaped upon us daily by our carers and how it was becoming too much to bear. These female supervisors were meant to be looking out for our best interests, but instead they made us feel as though we were a stain on society. We both agreed that we felt worthless and no-good for anything or to anyone. That very day, we planned to run away together as soon as an opportunity presented itself. All our outings were supervised, with one supervisor in the lead and one or two of them at the back of the group. We were about twenty girls in all. Once a fortnight, we walked into town to collect our dole money. All of our money, with the exception of fifty cents, was given to the 'Home' for our board and keep. I usually purchased two blocks of chocolate with the remaining money, which lasted me the two weeks.

On one of our outings, Wendy and I were walking side by side, discussing in low whispers once again, the idea of somehow escaping. We both concluded that it would be impossible, what with bars on the windows, outside lights on at night that lit up the entire surroundings, as well as other security measures set up to keep us inside. Then, it was as though we both saw it at the same time and had the exact same idea. There was a rowing boat anchored just a few feet from the beach, complete with a set of oars. Whispering excitedly to each other, we made plans to break from the group, run to the boat and row to the island we could see that looked to be not too far away from the shore.

'How far do you think it is from here?' I whispered to my friend.

'Only about three kilometres,' she replied. We agreed that it would be easy to row to freedom, away from the hateful situation we were in.

But it was not to be. One of the supervising ladies suspected that we were planning something and came and walked the rest of the way into town with us. Which was just as well. We later discovered the island we thought was within our capability to reach was in fact more than forty-four kilometres from the coast where we had planned to 'borrow' the boat. Also, the seas are treacherous in that area. So, it was in our best interest that our plans were thwarted. We actually saw the funny side of this when we imagined what we would have looked like rowing that old boat. We were both eight months pregnant at the time.

Another regular outing was our prenatal check-up at the local hospital. I dreaded going, as once again it was as though we were on display as the girls from '1 Shields Street', the home for unmarried mothers. We entered the maternity section of the hospital in pairs, accompanied by four supervisors. The other mothers made no secret of the way they felt about us; some whispering behind their hands to one another, and others even pointing unashamedly. It just added to the already low self-worth most of us carried with us, wherever we went. Even though I became good friends with a couple of the other girls, it did not take away the shame and hurt we all felt from the cruel remarks made daily by the staff at the home and other people with whom we came into contact.

I cried myself to sleep most nights in that dingy bedroom. I was so homesick for my family and hated myself for what I had put them through. I just wanted for this to be over so my baby and I could leave and go home. I especially missed my dad. The rules of the home stated female visitors only, one day per week. On the only occasion I had visitors, my mum and elder sister came to see me while Dad had to wait in the car. It broke my heart as I missed him so much. I totally understood that my family could not visit me more regularly due to their commitment to the dairy farm and the distance involved in driving to see me. My boyfriend and I kept in contact via post. He visited the home four or five times in the five months we were apart, despite the four-hour drive each way from the town where he resided. He was satisfied with just being able to wave to me from his car and for us to be able to blow kisses to each other before he was spotted by the staff and asked to move on.

In the delegated one hour resting time each day, I crocheted and knit beautiful clothes for my new baby. I made bootees, bonnets, dresses, little cardigans and a bunny rug. I was so proud of my work and excited, too, as my due date drew closer. I packed the clothes into a special bag and dreamed of how he or she would look in these garments I had made with such love in my heart. Finally, the big day arrived.

## Chapter Seven

## The Birth of My Son

### —1970—

*'The LORD is near to those who have a broken heart,
And saves such as have a contrite spirit'.*

—Psalm 34:18 —

Early in the morning on the ninth of April 1970, my contractions began. After having endured the past five months of ill treatment in the home, I was hoping that once inside the safety of the hospital, things would be different. But it was not to be. I was discriminated against by most of the staff in the same way I had been in the home. Once they realised that I was an unmarried mother, they looked upon me with utter disdain.

Certain preparations were carried out prior to me being taken to the labour ward, including an enema. I found the contractions even harder to cope with as the midwife roughly administered this procedure. When she had finished, she showed me where the bathroom was and informed me that if I could not make it there in time, I would be cleaning up the mess, regardless of how much pain I was experiencing.

All of the same condemnation that had already been spoken over me was repeated. She let me know she hoped I would suffer in the hours ahead as a punishment for the wrong I had, supposedly, done.

I was taken to the labour ward and left alone to cope the best way I could. As time passed, my contractions became stronger and occurred more regularly. Having been raised on a farm, my siblings and I were taught not to complain as such unless we were almost at death's door. I was quite tough in that regard and could normally put up with a lot. But I had never experienced pain like this before. Back at the 'home', we were instructed not to ask questions about the birth process, as it may 'frighten' us if we knew the details. Without knowing what to expect and given that I was so young, I was absolutely terrified as the contractions took control of my body. The midwife had warned me to only push the buzzer if absolutely necessary. After a couple of hours and the pain reaching the unbearable stage, I felt that this was about as necessary as you could get, so I called for help. I could tell by the midwife's demeanour as she walked towards the bed, that she was not happy with me. I pleaded with her for pain relief of some sort and my request was turned down. Without performing an examination, she told me I had hours to endure yet. She mumbled once again, something about the pain I was experiencing was my punishment and not to bother her by ringing the buzzer unnecessarily again.

I could not stand this any longer and scanned the room looking for some sort of cutting instrument. The only object I could see was a biro lying on a desk, just out of my reach. I looked at the veins running down the inside of my wrist, wondering if the biro point would be sharp enough to penetrate. I was desperate to find a way out so both my baby and I could pass from this world and end this horrendous suffering that I was sure he or she must have been going through also.

Later, when the midwife returned to see how my labour was progressing, a rather concerned look crossed her face as she checked my cervix and baby's heartbeat. She left the room in a hurry, returning shortly afterwards accompanied by a doctor and another female staff member. It was at this point that a change of shift took place. I did not see the first midwife for the rest of my stay in hospital. With the staff rotation came a change of attitude. The new staff showed respect and compassion at first, as they were obviously unaware that I was an unmarried mother. This was so different from the way I had been treated for the past five months. It was as though my heart was a dry sponge, soaking up the moisture of love and care that had been so lacking in my life of late.

The doctor administered a procedure in order for my baby to be born as quickly as possible, and my tiny son entered the world shortly afterwards. The new midwife wrapped him up and brought him to me briefly. When I saw him, I could hardly believe the miracle of this beautiful baby boy who had once been a part of me. I wished to hold him immediately, but she kindly explained that she needed to take him to another room, to weigh and clean him up a little. Before long she returned and placed my new baby into my arms. I will never forget how I felt as I looked upon his precious little face. The whole experience was indescribable. I wanted to leave right away, take him home and show him off to my family. Soon it would be just the two of us. Far from prying, gossiping and condemning people.

It was then I heard loud voices approaching the labour ward. I could tell by the tone that there was a matter of urgency at hand as they drew closer. I soon realised that I was their target. It was the hospital matron, accompanied by two nurses. The matron began shouting at the staff, demanding they take my baby from me as he was for adoption. Of course, I strongly objected, informing them they were mistaken.

What happened next was like a very bad dream. There began a tug of war with my precious little one. The staff tried to take him forcefully from my arms. I was screaming, my baby was screaming and so were

# THE BIRTH OF MY SON

the staff. I was forced to give in for my little one's sake. The nursing staff ripped him physically from my arms and at the same time it felt as though they had ripped out my very heart. I cannot describe the pain I felt. If you have been through this, you will understand.

But I thought they had only taken him for a little while. That, surely, they would come to their senses and realise their mistake. I was moved into a ward with three other new mothers to 'recover'; or so the staff told me. In those days, the babies were transported from the nursery to their mum's rooms, approximately every four hours via a long trolley. Nurses delivered them from the trolley in the hallway to each ward. After approximately one hour, the babies were collected again and taken back to the nursery where they remained till next feed time.

As the babies were brought to the other three mothers in my ward, I waited excitedly for the nurse to bring my baby to me. My heart sank, as, without a word, the trolley proceeded further along the hallway to the next ward. I went boldly to the nursery.

'I have come to collect my baby so I can feed him,' I explained to the nurse who answered the door.

'Oh no,' she exclaimed. 'Haven't you been told? Your baby is for adoption. All you need do before you are discharged tomorrow is sign the necessary paperwork'.

'You must be mistaken,' I replied. 'I haven't placed him for adoption. He is my baby and I am taking him home'.

The nurse muttered something about sending someone to speak with me as soon as possible.

I waited most of the day until a counsellor paid me a brief visit later that afternoon. She told me that my mother had phoned the hospital and asked the staff to give me this message. 'Don't even consider bringing your baby home to us, because if you do, you will no longer be a part of this family'. I did not believe my mother would say such a thing.

From then on, each time the babies were brought to the room I shared with the other ladies, I pulled the curtains around my bed so as not to witness them bonding. It was just too painful. The nurses would pull the curtains back again and tell me to sign the paperwork and I would be free to go. I could not bear to remain in the room so I went to the nursery instead, hoping to talk some sense into someone and explain to them that I did not and would not consent to my baby's adoption. The next day I was presented with adoption papers and informed that once I had signed them I would be free to leave the hospital. I refused point blank to sign the paperwork, (or even read it for that matter), telling the staff that I was taking my baby home. My breasts in the meantime had become swollen, hot and red as they became engorged with milk. I pleaded with the staff to give my baby to me so I could feed him. When they refused, I asked for some sort of medication to ease the pain and pressure.

They bargained with me, 'If you sign the adoption papers, you can have the medication to dry up your milk'.

Desperation took over and I decided to steal my baby and run away with him. Unfortunately, each time I attempted to enter the nursery to collect him, the door was locked. Because I was being so 'difficult', the hospital staff decided to punish me by moving me to a ward beside the nursery. From my new location, I could see the staff placing babies on the trolley for delivery to their mums, and I could hear my baby's cry. This truly broke my heart as I recognised his little voice, which caused my milk to 'come in'. My maternal instincts were in overdrive. This was so wrong. When I heard his cries, I would check to see if the curtains of the nursery were open. I longed to get a glimpse of him at least. Sometimes I was lucky enough to see one of the nurses attending to him. But as soon as she noticed me looking longingly into the nursery, she pulled the curtains closed again. Oh, how I yearned for him, longing for the staff to come to their senses and just give him to me. Then we could leave and go back to my family.

Each day, one of the staff placed adoption papers before me, pleading for me to sign them. I refused. All I asked was to take my baby home. I was determined not to leave the hospital without him. When my little one was one week old, a counsellor whom I had not met previously, came to my room with the same paperwork. As we sat either side of the hospital bed, she informed me that a lovely couple who were millionaires had come to visit and had chosen my baby to adopt. This counsellor seemed a little more understanding and compassionate as far as *my* needs were concerned. However, I answered her in the same way I had the others who had tried to talk me into placing my signature on the paperwork. I would not give permission for someone else to take my baby as their own.

She then quizzed me about how I intended to care for and support my son. What could I offer him? After all, I could not take him to my parents' house. My family had already made their feelings clear on the matter, she reminded me. 'Where will you live? What money do you have set aside? This wealthy family who so desperately wants your son can give him the best of everything. What can you offer in comparison?'

'I can give him love', I answered as she pushed the paperwork towards me. I was broken. She had finally found a way to blackmail me into giving up my baby. Because I loved him so much and wanted what was best for him, I signed the adoption papers. I was absolutely grief-stricken, knowing that even though I loved him, I could never match the material wealth this rich couple could, supposedly, lavish upon him.

Tears blinding my eyes, I reached into the locker beside my bed and withdrew the package of baby clothes I had made and began to unpack them. I had spent hours crocheting and knitting these beautiful garments in that wretched home for unmarried mothers. At least it was something I could give to my baby from me. I took the folded garments from the packaging and passed them across the bed to the previously compassionate counsellor, asking her to please give them to my baby's adoptive parents.

But now that she had my signature on the paperwork, she looked at me and scoffed, 'What would they want with these?'

It was as though she was thinking that the contents of the package before her, was some sort of trash I had pulled from a bin somewhere. I stood and walked around to her side of the hospital bed, and began to carefully unfold each garment, placing them before her. It was as though I was trying to prove myself to her somehow. That I was not the person she was trying to make me out to be.

'They wouldn't want them', she snapped, turning her head so as not to even glance at the layette on the bed in front of her. 'Donate them to the hospital on your way out. You are now free to leave'.

I did not think I could ever feel more broken than I felt then. This woman's cruel reaction to the clothing I had so lovingly made for my baby was almost too much to bear. The clothes were not good enough, and neither was I.

My heart was crushed and my spirit broken as I walked slowly from the hospital. I could not begin to fathom how, in the last half hour or so, I had been tricked into relinquishing my own baby. I will go as far as to say here that he was stolen from me. I had no legal team, no rights, it seemed, and no one to stand by me. I felt so alone. Words cannot explain the trauma of having your baby taken from you and the utter helplessness you feel. I was his mother, I had given birth to him, he belonged to me and now they had stolen him. The treatment I had endured for the past five months, (not to mention the emotional pain from being isolated from family and friends) was not even fitting for someone who had committed a terrible crime. I walked from that hospital, feeling as though I had just been handed a life sentence.

(If only I had known Jesus back then. I had no idea that He is equally near to all persons at all times. No matter what they are going through.)

## Chapter Eight

## In Search of Truth

### —1970-1978—

My parents came to pick me up and we drove back home to New South Wales in silence. I should have been excited to see our newly completed beachside house when we finally arrived, but instead, I felt lonely and more sad than I had ever felt before. I sat in my new bedroom and the emotional pain from having my child taken, so wrongfully, from me, enveloped me like a heavy blanket. It was like a weight I could not seem to lift. I was grieving for my precious baby and what could have been. There was no counselling available that I was aware of at the time, as way back then, you were told never to speak of such things and to forget they had ever happened. But because I could not vent the way I was feeling, I stuffed my pain deep down into some area of my being and rebelled against my parents.

I foolishly put my life in danger almost weekly and can hardly believe that I survived. Lynne and I continued to hitchhike, often accepting lifts in motor vehicles with drivers who were obviously under the influence of alcohol, drugs or both. Sometimes I lied to my parents about my whereabouts. We did lots of other crazy and dangerous things and I now believe that because of my mum and dad's faithful prayers for my safety, God was protecting me. Even though I was acting as though He did not even exist. As a consequence of my rebellious ways, I brought even more suffering on myself. I was, in fact, self-harming again, in a way, trying to forget the past, but at the same time, craving attention. I could not stand being alone due to the memories that flooded my mind of the overwhelming love I had felt for my son when I held him for that precious one and only time. I also recalled the injustice, trickery, lies and manipulation that were used in order to take him from me.

Time did not seem to be erasing the grief I was experiencing, but life continues regardless of how we are coping. So, I threw myself into it head long, doing everything in my power to forget the past six months. It was the '70s and the height of the hippie, surfie eras. Lynne and I considered ourselves to be a little of both. We hung out around the beaches of Byron Bay and Brunswick Heads, often hitchhiking at night to dances which were located forty odd kilometres from home. Some of the popular bands we listened to at the time were the Beatles, The Beach Boys and Creedence Clearwater Revival.

Meanwhile, my boyfriend and I were still dating, and we decided to get married nine months after the birth of my son. I was three months pregnant at our wedding. We loved each other, and in the '70s. it was not unusual for people from that era to marry at a young age. My husband's work required us to move quite often throughout New South Wales and Queensland, so we decided to purchase a caravan.

As time went on, my thoughts were still consumed with my baby boy and I often daydreamed about the day I would meet him. I wondered how old he would be when that wonderful day actually came to pass. I pondered the idea of perhaps, somehow just catching a glimpse of him; just to know that he was safe, happy and well. Would that be enough to satisfy me? Or would it only make my emotional pain even worse? I prayed to God to bring this about. I found myself seeking out any stationary pram that was occupied by a baby boy who appeared to be around the same age as my son would be. I must have appeared almost manic, as a lot of parents moved their prams, along with their precious cargo away from me and closer to themselves. Upon realising I had probably given the appearance of being a 'baby napper', I would try to explain my way out of the situation by making up some story or another about how cute I thought their child was.

My husband was exceptionally good to me, but he loved to drink alcohol as though the brewery was about to run dry. After work each day, he went to the pub for a few hours with his work mates. Because I spent so much time alone, my mind became an open door for thoughts of my past to consume me. I began to feel as though I was driven and did everything to excess. If I kept busy with cleaning the van, exercising, cooking and preparing for the arrival of our new little one, there was not much time left to face myself. A self I did not particularly like.

Our first baby was born on the 21$^{st}$ of July 1971. She was beautiful, but I was in shock as I did not have a clue about how to care for her. There was no such thing back then as a midwife coming to visit you a day or two after you had given birth to make sure that you were coping. I do not know how she survived except, thanks be to God, instinct prevailed (mostly) and we settled into a routine. Thirteen months later, a gorgeous little sister for my daughter came into the world. Life certainly was busy now. But at least this time I had a better idea of how to care for our second little one. We continued to move from state to state, residing in caravan parks in towns closest to where my husband was working. I actually began to enjoy the lifestyle, often meeting other families, some of whom had babies around the same age as our little ones.

It was in one of these Caravan Parks that I met a lady who introduced me to the Ouija board. She and I took great delight in asking ridiculous questions of supposed spirits and watching almost spellbound as an upturned glass moved around the board to certain letters of the alphabet, spelling out the answers to our questions. I had no idea that what we were participating in 'just for fun' was not only dangerous but also demonic. We were dabbling in the occult. My new friend told me that her mother was a well-known medium who lived in another state of Australia. After speaking to her via the telephone one day, her mother advised us to stop mucking around with the Ouija board, as great harm could come upon not only us, but our loved ones as well. We took her advice but then began to seek the help of clairvoyants, mediums and palm readers in order to find the answers to life that we both were seeking. But our search through these avenues was, of course, in vain.

After my husband and I had been married approximately three years, he built us a comfortable brick home in North Queensland. Because he was such a skilful bricklayer, he was guaranteed work in the area for many years to come. Despite the fact that I had made good friends, I was growing more and more restless as the days went by, thinking that there had to be more to life than what I was experiencing in my part of the world. I realise now that I had married way too young and the responsibilities of two little ones, with no help from my husband, was taking its toll. I longed for him to come home to us after work, instead of sitting and drinking with the 'boys' half the night. But I never communicated to him just how unhappy I was. Instead, I became more and more resentful about what I saw as him putting his mates before his family.

I did not know how to communicate how I was feeling. I never expressed how I felt after my son was taken from me either. As a child, my siblings and I were not allowed to speak much about how we were feeling about anything, really. We were told to 'buck up' if we even looked a little bit down. In other words, get over it, whatever it was. Unfortunately, this became a pattern in my life which I passed on to my family.

Not long after my 21st birthday, I decided to leave my husband and take our two small girls with me. Probably not the best decision I have ever made in my life. I was not even willing to try to work things out with him. I did not know how to, or where to start. I found out years later that because I never expressed concern about why he spent so much time with friends and so little time with us, he thought I did not care for him. Because I had never communicated to him about how lonely I was and how unhappy I was feeling, he was understandably shocked by my decision to leave. Our little girls and I moved to a share house with a friend who also had two daughters around the same ages as mine.

Not long after we separated, our youngest daughter became ill with an infection. She began to fit and was rushed to hospital, where she was admitted and diagnosed with septicaemia. My husband and I were told at first to expect the worst. But then her condition seemed to improve for a short period of time and she was allowed home. It was not long, though, before the infection recurred and several times afterwards, she was admitted to hospital with the same symptoms. After many months of trying to find answers from many different doctors and specialists, and several courses of antibiotics later, my little girl's first teeth turned yellow. Out of desperation I then sought the help of a naturopath who appeared to heal her within weeks. He did this by simply changing her diet and prescribing the use of certain herbal remedies. I was astounded. After witnessing this sudden change, I became obsessed with healthy eating.

My friend whom I shared a house with, worked at a fairly up-market hotel in the main street of town. I asked her if she could enquire for me to see if there were any positions vacant. My only experience in the hotel industry was when I had participated in a three-week bar course a few years previously. To my surprise, her boss phoned and arranged an appointment for an interview. Immediately after the interview, he asked whether I would be available to begin work the very next week in the cocktail bar. I had exaggerated, telling him I could mix at least twenty-four different cocktails and knew all of the recipes off by heart. I needed to arrange a babysitter, purchase a cocktail book and begin studying. I was genuinely concerned now, that I had not told the truth and had talked myself up too much. During my three-week bar course, I had only been shown how to pour soapy water from a beer tap in order to learn to create a 'good head' on a glass of beer. The sum total of my learning to mix a few cocktails, was practising using coloured water, cream and ice, in a cocktail shaker. I felt like such a phoney.

So, I began my 'fake it until you make it' job in the cocktail bar. My good friend minded my little girls whilst I waited to receive a response from an advertisement I had placed in the local paper for a reliable babysitter. One afternoon after work, I returned home to see our front veranda crowded with people, all of whom had come in response to my advertisement. One at a time I carefully interviewed them, wondering why I was beginning to feel nauseous. I could not trust any of these people with my children. I had almost given up hope by the time I got to the last two applicants. They were an older retired couple with grandchildren of their own. They explained that they loved children and a little bit of extra pocket money would come in handy in order to supplement their income. Instantly I knew they would be perfect for the job. As time went on, the girls grew to love them and referred to them as 'Nanna' and 'Pop'. And you would not believe it. I ended up becoming manageress of the cocktail bar six months later.

But while my daughters were safely in the care of this older couple, I began experimenting with drugs and alcohol in order to fill the emptiness I still felt inside. My heartache for my son was still as raw as the day he had been taken from me. I also felt guilty for taking my little girls from their father as I witnessed his deep sadness each time he visited them. Alcohol and drugs temporarily numbed my guilt and shame, but when the effects of such wore off, nothing had changed. I also began my old pattern of seeking answers from fortune-tellers and tarot card readers as I searched blindly for Truth.

It was around this time that the obsession I had with eating healthy food escalated out of control. In those days I had never heard of eating disorders, but I now know that I was bulimic. This horrid disorder ruled my life for at least three to four years. In those days, fasting for long periods of time and 'do it yourself' enemas were also popular methods to boost one's health. I did both, with my longest fast being three weeks, at the end of which I felt amazing. But I was obsessively over the top with anything that could possibly change the way I was and the way I looked. I ate ridiculously small portions of fresh raw foods throughout the day, but in the evenings, I craved something sweet. To satisfy this urge, I snacked on chocolate and ice cream which caused me to feel guilty because I had eaten unhealthy food. So, I would immediately make myself sick by sticking my fingers down my throat and throwing up until I was certain there was nothing left in my tummy. Nobody else was aware of my secret.

It had been four years since my son was taken from me and it was obvious that I was still suffering from the trauma of being separated from him. I was growing more desperate by the day to find him. But desperation sometimes drives one to do crazy things. One day I decided to phone a department linked to adoptions and I spoke to a male person. (Maybe a social worker. I cannot remember for sure.) Many conversations later with the same man, I imagined he and I had become 'mates'. I decided to take a risk and bribe him into disclosing the address of my son's adoptive parents, offering him $630 I had saved, specifically for this purpose. If I had an address, I could just drive to the street where he lived, and sit somewhere up the road out of sight, hopefully catching a glimpse of him. Or I could at least ask someone who lived in the same area about the family.

I went ahead with my plan, but my 'friend' threatened to tell the authorities of my attempted bribe. I had hit a dead end. I did not give up, though, and for a couple of years I placed advertisements in a magazine called 'Pix,' in a section printed for the Salvation Army. This was specifically for anyone wishing to discover the whereabouts of friends or family with whom they had lost contact. From memory I advertised the only information I had about my son – his date of birth and the hospital where he was born but to no avail.

In the meantime, I felt very unsettled and decided to move back to New South Wales. I found accommodation in the same seaside village where my friend Lynne and her husband resided, and before long, I was employed at a hotel right next to the small unit I rented for the girls and me. But even though I had changed address and loved spending time with my little girls and my friends, I still felt lonely. I was continually seeking something that would fill the emptiness I was feeling. My husband wanted to attempt to mend our relationship, but I was not interested. I was sick mentally, too busy working and obsessed with health and exercise. My body image became a daily challenge, as I slipped deeper and deeper towards rock bottom.

That was until I began dating another man. He was a lecturer at a university near the town where I was residing at the time. Perhaps he could make me feel better about myself? He certainly was full of compliments. But the relationship was yet another failure, as I realised fairly quickly that he was also dating several of his female students. I moved back to Brunswick Heads to be near my parents. Years later, memories of the past consumed me to the point that I knew I had no choice but to seek professional help. When I told my older daughters that I was attending counselling sessions once a week, they could not understand why I needed to do this. I explained to them that I felt like a failure because I had experienced so many failed relationships and that during one counselling session, I disclosed that I had been sexually abused as a child. The girls then told me that when we were living with the university lecturer and they were four and five years old, he had touched both of them inappropriately on one occasion. My immediate reaction was to call the authorities and have him charged, but my daughters agreed that they would just rather forget about it.

## Chapter Nine

## Domestic Violence

## —1978-1980—

At the beginning, I felt settled and happy residing in the same beachside town as my parents. I rented a small upstairs flat above the local health food shop, which was ideal, given the fact that I was still obsessed with us consuming healthy food. Because I was such a frequent customer, I became quite friendly with the owner of the shop. Between us we began a barter system, whereby I exchanged homemade yoghurt, freshly baked bread and other healthy homemade treats for whatever organic produce or supplements my daughters and I required at the time. My children were now seven and eight years old and loved the fact we now lived in such close proximity to their grandparents.

I made sure we took a trip at least twice per year from New South Wales to Queensland, in order for the girls to spend time with their father and for me to catch up with friends. We caught a bus to Brisbane and then continued on our journey via rail to Cairns. The train trip took approximately 32 hours in those days and was very entertaining due to some of the unusual characters we met along the way, especially in the dining car. On arrival at our destination, we were exhausted but happy to see everybody over the next couple of weeks and exchange stories about what we had been doing since we were last together. My ex-husband and I had many mutual friends with children around the same age as our girls, and we usually arranged to meet them at one of the local hotels.

It was at one of these meetings that I noticed a man selling tickets in a chook raffle. When he approached the table I was at with my friends, I purchased a ticket and observed that he was quite good looking. He had thick curly black hair with dark brown eyes and olive skin. After I paid for the ticket, he struck up a conversation with me. We talked for some time and he told me that he was on holiday. Immediately after he had left, my ex-husband came to caution me not to have anything to do with the ticket seller, as he apparently had a bad reputation. My ex had warned me several times previously about *any* man who showed interest in me, so I thought it was more a warning out of jealousy than anything else. I took no heed to his words.

Before I left the hotel with the children, the man, whom I will call Tom, approached me and asked me on a date. I could see no harm in this, so I went out with him that very night. We seemed to get on well together, and during the following week, we caught up for dinner on another couple of occasions prior to the end of his holiday. I began to feel a close connection to Tom, and he told me he felt the same way towards me. Before he left Cairns, we decided to meet again in Brisbane. This was where he resided with his parents and five brothers. Not long after the girls and I had arrived back home, I arranged to leave my children with their grandparents while I travelled to Brisbane to see him. I met his mother and father, his brothers and one of his brother's wives. They all seemed very nice and friendly. From then on, I visited Tom quite frequently, and on the last couple of occasions, I took my girls along. It was on one of these visits that he asked me if we could move in together.

He did not have to ask twice. I thought Tom was lovely. He appeared to be a non-drinker, a natural with children and was very loving and kind towards me. And I really liked his family, even though his five brothers seemed a little rough at times. We decided to move to Townsville and begin our lives together there. I packed up our little flat, bid my very nervous parents goodbye and caught a bus from Brunswick heads to Brisbane, with my girls and a couple of suitcases. The next day we were to catch the bus to Townsville.

When we arrived at the bus depot the next morning, I received quite a shock when Tom introduced me to two men who were also waiting for the same bus we were about to board. He explained that they were his mates and were coming to Townsville with us. He said that this would help us out by them contributing towards the rent once we had found a suitable place to live. I was not happy about this arrangement initially, but the excitement I felt at the thought of the girls and me beginning a new season in our lives with this wonderful man soon caused me to forget my previous discomfort.

Once our journey began, the bus made several rest stops, along the way to Townsville. Most of the passengers took advantage of these intermittent breaks, except for Tom's friends who remained on the bus, appearing to be asleep. I found this rather odd, but when I mentioned my concern to Tom, he told me that his mates were very tired and were catching up on their sleep. As I was getting back on the bus with the girls after one of the rest breaks, I noticed several people approaching the coach driver and could not help but overhear their conversations. They were complaining that some of their belongings were missing from where they had stowed them in the overhead luggage racks. The driver did not seem to have an answer for them as to how this could have happened, and so we continued on our way, finally arriving in Townsville the next morning.

Our first priority was to find accommodation, so we inquired at several rental establishments, and finally found a cheap, fully self-contained, three-bedroom old 'Queenslander'. It had a driveway down the side and a nice big backyard where the children could play. Once we unloaded our luggage, we discovered a supermarket nearby, purchased some supplies and cooked dinner. After dinner, Tom's friends headed out 'somewhere'. It had been such a busy day that the children, Tom and I retired early for the night. The sound of a vehicle driving down the side of our house woke me in the early hours of the morning. I looked out the window and noticed Tom's friends alighting from a white station wagon. Something did not seem quite right about this. I woke Tom and asked him what his friends would be doing with a vehicle which, in the half-dark, looked as though it was packed to the roof with something. After glancing briefly out the window himself, Tom didn't seem bothered at all and told me not to worry and to go back to sleep. He said that his mates had probably just done a 'bust'. I had never heard of a 'bust' before, so I asked him what that meant.

Tom could not believe that I had never heard of such a thing. He told me that it was when you break in and steal something. He said that by the looks of the car and its contents, that his mates had robbed more than one place, as well as stealing the vehicle. I had only stolen one thing in my entire life and that was a bottle of nail polish when I was eleven years old. I felt so guilty at the time that I returned to the shop the next day and attempted to place it back on the shelf. That silly bottle of polish was harder to put back than it was to steal in the first place. The shopkeeper kept eyeing me suspiciously, so the minute she was distracted by another customer, I replaced the bottle and fled. I must have looked so awkward.

I was beside myself once the realisation hit me that there was a stolen car in the backyard of the house we had rented the previous day, full of stolen property. I couldn't sleep, so at first light I woke Tom again and told him that we had to do something about this situation. Due to the urgency and panic in my voice, my girls awoke and joined us. Tom's friends had obviously retired, after their busy night.

Tom went downstairs to check out the stolen goods inside the car. When he returned, he calmly handed each of my girls a small transistor radio. He said it looked as though his friends had 'done over' a radio station, jewellery store and several other places going on what he could see amongst the contents of the car. I pleaded with him to remove the stolen vehicle from our yard and take it to the nearest police station, so the police would find it and return it to its owner, without too much trouble. He looked at me like I was from another planet. He explained that if we took the car anywhere near a police station, we would quite likely be caught and implicated in the thefts. My thought was just to get the car away from our dwelling. So, after much badgering on my part, Tom drove the car along with the girls and me and began to head out of town. His intention was to dump it and its contents as far away from a police station as he could.

As we were driving along one of the streets, we noticed a taxi approaching us from the opposite direction. Tom observed the driver reach for his two-way radio and explained to me that the cab driver was probably alerting the police or the taxi company of the stolen vehicle. In my naivety, once again I suggested that instead of the police bothering to come and find us, why didn't we just take the car to them. But before he could answer, the sound of sirens cut the air. Tom took off and there we were, my innocent little girls and I, in the middle of a high-speed police chase. Tom drove like a maniac, up and down one-way streets, back streets and every which way, trying to lose our pursuers. In a 'last ditch' attempt, he headed back to our flat, intending to conceal the car in the backyard, but to no avail. As we began to pull into our driveway, a police vehicle pulled across in front of us, blocking our entry.

I felt so guilty for my little girls' sake as a policewoman grabbed me roughly from the vehicle and threw me against the side fence of the driveway. She demanded I drop my bag on the ground and raise my arms above my head as she proceeded to search me. I cried tears of shame that this was actually happening. But there was much more to come. I turned to see how my little daughters were coping with this terrible situation and to reassure them that I was alright. They had fled the scene and were now running up the stairs, seemingly set on getting inside quickly. I assumed that they were frightened and were simply heading for safety. My girls were inside the flat before the other law enforcement officers even had a chance to enter. Once the police lady was satisfied that I had nothing on my person and there wasn't anything of interest to her in my bag, I ran upstairs to witness Tom's friends being pulled from their beds, forcefully. The police appeared to know them very well. I was shocked to hear that, in fact, these two men had both been released from a Brisbane jail the week prior to our travelling to Townsville.

They had been incarcerated for four years for armed robbery. I recalled the bus trip and passengers complaining to the coach driver about certain items missing from their hand luggage the previous night. That is why those men had remained on the bus. Goodness only knows what they had stolen. While Tom's friends were being questioned, my two little girls sat very quietly on the sofa. I sat with them in shock and watched as our flat was torn apart by the police. Drawers were pulled from wardrobes and cupboards, their contents upended, searched and left in a heap. One very astute policewoman noticed the linoleum was slightly raised on the kitchen floor. She proceeded to pull it back and discovered a number of stolen passports, licenses and other paperwork. On searching the contents of the car, the police found jewellery, radios, cartons of cigarettes and lots more stolen property. The two men had had a busy night, so it seemed. They were taken to the watch house to await court and sentencing the following day.

After the police finally left, I realised that my little girls had been sitting on the small transistor radios they had been 'gifted' from part of the loot. Do you know that I honestly cannot remember whether I handed those radios in or not? It was such a stressful time that I have forgotten a lot of what happened. The police returned to our flat for at least the next five days, still searching for other stolen items they had obviously been unable to locate. Each time after they had finished their search, I was left to re-pack the contents of drawers and cupboards they had pulled apart. I became so tired of putting things back, that by about the third day, I left everything where they had thrown it, until I knew for certain that they would not be back. As far as I can remember, Tom's friends were sentenced and sent back to jail. I didn't realise at this time that I had actually fallen for a man who was known to police and had also spent many years in prison for armed robbery and other crimes he had committed.

We moved to another rental property in Townsville and I enrolled my girls in school. We had only resided there for a week or two, when, one evening, Tom suggested that he and I go for a drink before dinner to a hotel across the road. Seeing as we lived so close, I thought it would be ok to leave the girls for a short time. It was nice to be alone together after all the drama we had just been through. But we had only consumed one drink each when Tom began to accuse me of flirting with two men sitting across the bar from us. I assured him that I had not even noticed them until he brought them to my attention. He ordered himself another drink which he then skulled as though it was water. This was the first occasion I had ever witnessed him drinking alcohol.

Suddenly, I began to feel sick in my stomach. It was as though I had a premonition that something very bad was about to take place. I asked Tom if we could leave and go back to my children. But he had already ordered a third drink, which he also drank straight down. He then turned toward me and the look on his face frightened me. His whole persona had changed. His breathing became heavy and his nostrils flared as he glared at me. His eyes were as black as coal and the veins in his neck bulged. I was terrified, and in my haste to return to my girls, I attempted to snatch our house keys from the counter in front of him, accidently dropping them onto the floor. As I bent to retrieve the keys, he grabbed me by the hair and pulled me up with such force, my head hit the wooden rail of the bar. I was stunned. I turned and tried to run, but he caught hold of me by the tie at the front of the sarong I was wearing.

I struggled to free myself from him, glancing briefly at the two men across the bar, pleading with my eyes for them to step in and help me. But instead, they stared in shock and disbelief. Tom dragged me into the street and across the road. My little girls on hearing that we had arrived home, came excitedly at first, to greet us. I told them to go back to their room, but Tom insisted they stay. Their eyes filled with fear when they saw the wild look on his face and witnessed how terrified *I* was. They turned to run but Tom insisted that they remain where they were and watch what happens to a mother as bad as me. He made me sit in a chair, then proceeded to tell my beautiful children dreadful lies about me. He called me horrible and degrading names and began to smoke one cigarette after another, finishing each one and butting them out on my thighs. I remained silent. He then pulled me to my feet, pulled his arm back and with a full fist, punched me in the face. I don't remember much except seeing blood spurt all over the wall.

The next thing I remember was Tom carrying me into a bedroom furnished with two old fashioned heavy wardrobes, a dressing table and a double and single bed. He commanded my girls to lie on the single bed as he placed me on the double bed beside them. He then barricaded us into the room with the wardrobes, and in front of my precious children, he raped me, then fell asleep. The girls and I were frozen with fear. We were so frightened that we dared not even whisper to each other. One of my daughters reached across the gap between the beds, took hold of one of my hands and held it, squeezing it throughout the night, as though to comfort me.

The following day when Tom awoke, he looked at me and began to cry. He asked me who had hurt me and who was responsible for barricading us in the room. He took a damp face cloth and tenderly cleaned the dry blood from my face and nostrils. He told me my nose had been broken and that I required medical attention. I could not speak. I was in shock. He took me to a doctor's surgery just down the street from our rental house. I was terrified of him, even though he was being so kind to me now. When the doctor asked what happened, I lied and said that I had accidentally run into a wall. He gave Tom a very angry glance and sent me to the hospital for treatment.

Immediately after I left the hospital, a very strange thing happened that I now believe was God intervening in my life, to save my children and me from this very bad situation. Even though I was not in a close relationship with Him at this present time, I did know and believe in God's existence from what I had learnt when I attended Church and Sunday school as a child. A friend of my ex-husband's just happened to be standing outside the hospital. He was shocked when he saw my injuries. He asked me what had happened, and when I hesitated to answer him, he suggested that I had more than likely been involved in a very bad car accident. To which I agreed. At this stage, I had an inner knowing that if I were to reveal information to anyone regarding our situation, police or otherwise, my children and I could be killed.

I could tell Tom suspected I was going to try to take the children and flee, as he would not let me out of his sight.

About two months later at around three am one morning, I woke to the sound of police pounding on the door and demanding entry. When Tom opened the door, the police burst into the front room and said they had received a report from their fellow workers in Cairns, that a female had been assaulted at our address. I denied all knowledge of such a thing, lying to police and telling them that they must have the wrong information. I did not find out until years later, that the friend of my ex-husband's who had spoken to me outside the hospital had returned to Cairns and told my ex that he believed I had been the victim of domestic violence. My ex-husband apparently then reported this to the police. In the case of my relationship with Tom, the only emotion I felt towards him now was fear.

As you read the next two chapters, you may wonder why I did not take my children and flee, as several times I had the opportunity to do so. Tom began to threaten me that if I ever escaped and he was sent to jail, his brothers would kill my children, my precious family and me and anyone else who attempted to protect us. I believed him. He told me that his brothers knew 'how to deal with us'. They had done 'stuff' before, so the violence continued every time Tom decided to take a drink. We did escape on several occasions to friends and family, but due to the fear of the threats Tom had made, we surrendered to him each time he discovered our whereabouts.

I pleaded with God to provide an opportunity for my children and me to escape in such a way that my family and friends would not suffer the consequences. This man was a criminal with a history of violence and armed robbery, and I was not willing to take any chances.

# Chapter Ten

## Domestic Violence Continued

One evening after Tom had consumed copious amounts of alcohol, he beat me then proceeded to burn most of our belongings in a fire which he started in the lounge room of our rental home. I remember watching with my girls as their toys and most of their clothing turned to ash. The image of their broken little faces as they witnessed what little they owned and treasured being destroyed is etched deeply into my memory. Tom then burnt most of *my* clothing and anything else that he knew I valued. I remember three pretty blouses my mum had sent to me by post, that had belonged to my grandmother. I cherished these beautiful tops and gently hand washed them when necessary, as they were so old and delicate. My favourite was a pretty apricot coloured blouse with covered buttons down the front. As my children and I looked on in fear, we cried and clung to each other. How the house did not catch on fire, I will never know.

The next afternoon Tom assaulted me again. By some miracle I managed to escape with only my shoulder bag and ran blindly to the school with no thought as to how I must have looked. I hid behind a huge tree inside the school grounds in case Tom had followed me, waiting for school to finish. When I saw the girls approaching, I attracted their attention and we hid, until I was sure it was safe for us to leave the school grounds. We walked cautiously for about one kilometre until we came to a truck stop, all the while checking behind us, in case we were being followed. Outside, there were several semi-trailers and for some reason I felt drawn to seek shelter in one particular truck. I climbed onto the step, checked the passenger door and discovered it was unlocked. I pushed the girls into the cab, then hauled myself in behind them and shut the door.

Oh, the look of shock on the owner's face when he returned to his truck and found us huddled together like frightened rabbits. He ordered us out of the cab, but as I turned to look at him, my clothing covered in blood, both eyes blackened, my lip split and swollen, colour drained from his face as though he had just seen a ghost. He started the truck and without speaking a word, drove out of the service station and headed north. It was several minutes before he asked me what had happened. I didn't go into too much detail, as I was in a state of shock. When we reached the next town, the driver stopped and made a phone call from a pay phone, then without speaking a word, we continued on our way.

We drove until around midnight I think, and he insisted he take us to his home. The truck driver's wife, who was a complete stranger to us, greeted my girls and me as though we were her long-lost friends. She compassionately and oh so gently bathed my wounds, ran a warm bath for my daughters, cooked us a meal and invited us to stay for the night. I don't remember the circumstances surrounding our departure the next day, but I do know that I did not wish to put the lives of these 'good Samaritans' in danger, so we moved on. My little girls and I hitchhiked to Cairns and hired a cab to drive us to our friend's house. We were only there a couple of hours when Tom arrived. He must have guessed I would come back to my friends and possibly my ex-husband, for help.

He later boasted to me about how easy it had been to find us. He said he had approached several cab drivers and shown photos of his 'poor sister' and her two little girls and asked if any of them had seen us, as he was very worried for our wellbeing. He told them that someone had supposedly beaten his 'sister' and that she had run away, taking her children with her. The driver who had taken us to our friend recognised us from the photo, believed Tom's story and drove him to where we were. As soon as I saw Tom arrive, I picked up our belongings, and while my girlfriend tried to plead with me not to leave, I walked straight past her with my girls, and left with him in the cab. I knew that I could not put my friend and her family's lives at risk for trying to shelter us.

This was the way things were for a while. The girls and I escaped, went into hiding but surrendered each time Tom discovered our whereabouts. Unfortunately, each time we escaped, he became more aware that in order to keep us captive, he needed to stay closer and keep a better eye on his prey. He also began reminding me daily that his brothers would kill my family and me in the event he was sent back to jail, explaining in detail how they would carry this out. I believed Tom, as his brothers had visited us on numerous occasions and had witnessed him savagely beating me for no reason. They did nothing to prevent him from doing this. Not only that, they openly discussed in front of me how they would 'fix up' anyone who caused their brother to be sent back to jail.

Sometimes Tom didn't consume alcohol for weeks at a time and it was in these moments that he tried to be loving and kind to the girls and me. He took us fishing and crabbing, attempting to win us over in the hope that we would forget the trauma he had inflicted on us. But it wasn't enough. Nothing could blot out the memories of the horror he had put us through.

One night his brothers arrived unannounced with cartons of alcohol. Tom actually asked them to leave, as he said he was trying to stay sober. But after much badgering they convinced him to join them 'just for a few beers and a game of cards'. As soon as he opened his first drink, he insisted I stay in close proximity to him. I am sure he could sense the adrenalin as it coursed through my body, much like a shark who senses and draws near to a fish in distress. It wasn't long before Tom accused me of flirting with one of his brothers. He knocked me to the floor in full view of his siblings, dragged me to our balcony, picked me up by my ankles and lowered me over the railing. I was terrified he would drop me. His brothers could see what he was doing yet continued playing cards as though nothing unusual was happening, calling him when it was his turn to play and telling him to 'hurry up'. With that, he pulled me back up onto the balcony and continued the game, insisting I remain seated beside him. The assaults were becoming more frequent and each one greater in ferocity.

On another occasion, we had just finished grocery shopping and happened to be passing a bottle shop, when Tom decided to buy a carton of beer. Immediately upon arriving home, he began to drink. As I packed the groceries away, I could hear him mumbling insults about me. Because I was so nervous about the possibility of being assaulted in front of my children, yet again, I began to shake, accidentally dropping a couple of items as I continued with my task. This seemed to irritate him, so he came to the kitchen and began shoving me. The shoving escalated into a full-on assault, his fists beating me relentlessly. It was as though I shut down as this was taking place. I don't remember where the girls were, but suddenly the assault ceased. Instead Tom began yelling at me, calling me a 'copper dobber', shouting obscenities about police and reminding me of just how much he and his brothers hated them.

Before long, the police were actually banging loudly on our door demanding entry. Our neighbours had obviously called them and as strange as this may seem, I was not relieved by their presence. Instead, I felt nothing but dread. Tom would accuse me of somehow alerting them, which is crazy because he never let me out of his sight. The police would try to talk me into having him charged which I would not do under any circumstances, due to the reasons I have already mentioned. When they saw the state I was in, they pleaded with me to press charges. I refused. I agreed, however, to them escorting the children and me to a women's refuge. It was whilst I was there that I contacted my parents and revealed to them that the girls and I were in a bit of trouble. My mum sounded very worried, so I played down the whole situation about what was really happening and promised her I would keep in more regular contact.

The carers at the refuge were amazing. I made up my mind after the first week that once this nightmare was over and we had fully recovered, I would pursue work in this field. My desire was to give back to others who found themselves in a similar situation to the one we were currently experiencing, the love, care and support that was being lavished upon us. After we had been in the shelter for approximately three weeks, I asked one of the carers if it would be possible for me to go to the corner store to purchase some treats for my girls. The police had advised the manageress of the shelter, not to allow me to go anywhere. At first my request was turned down, but after giving further thought to the matter, she changed her mind and said she could see no harm in it. After all, it had been some weeks now with no threat from the 'perpetrator'. I could go to the shop so long as I was accompanied by one of the staff members and my girls remained in the shelter.

I relished the feeling of freedom as we walked less than a block to the corner shop. I noticed a phone booth immediately outside the store and remembered the promise I had made to my mum a couple of weeks previously. I asked permission to make a phone call. The staff member readily agreed to my request, as she said she could keep an eye on me from inside the shop. I placed some coins into the pay phone and dialled my parents' number. The next thing I remember is somebody's hand covering my mouth and being dragged from the phone booth to a car with the motor still running. I was pushed roughly into the passenger seat and forced into a horizontal position, as the person held me down. He then slammed the passenger door, slid across my body to the driver's side of the car and sat on my head in order to prevent me from moving.

Tom drove for what seemed like about twenty minutes. Once he stopped the car and finally released my head from under his backside, I opened the door and attempted to escape, frantically running from him. He caught up with me, dragged me inside an abandoned house and proceeded to beat me until I had no strength left to fight him off. Then he sexually assaulted me. Tom continued this behaviour for three days as payback for me being a 'friend of the police'. A 'copper dobber' as he called it. I don't remember him offering me food or drink, but I do remember the beatings and repeated sexual assaults. I was assaulted so badly that I don't know to this day, how I lived through it. On the third day, he dragged me to the car and sat on my head as he had previously. He had stripped me naked this time, thinking that would prevent me from escaping. We drove for what seemed like fifteen minutes when suddenly he stopped at a set of lights. I knew we were in the city somewhere, as I could hear heavy traffic and the ticking noise the lights make for handicapped people in order for them to know when it is safe to cross the road. Without even thinking about it, suddenly 'something' took over my entire body. I say 'something', or some kind of supernatural strength, because otherwise I could not possibly have done what I did next.

I kicked the passenger door open and at the same time reefed my head from underneath Tom's buttocks. I ran into the closest shop not even aware of my nakedness. I still remember the shocked expression on the young girl's face who stood behind the reception desk. I also remember very clearly the elderly ladies, about four or five of them, sitting sedately in a row, heads under old-fashioned egg-shaped hair driers, waiting for their freshly done hair dos to dry as they read the latest gossip magazines. Obviously, this was a hairdressing salon, and I can only imagine their shock when they saw me. When you are in the state I was in, you don't think about your appearance or even the fact you are naked. The only thing you are concentrating on is your fight for survival. Your will to stay alive.

The receptionist called the police and I was taken to hospital. Once again, I did not press charges due to my ongoing fear. I don't remember how long after this we left the shelter, or the events leading up to Tom finding us once more. But I knew for certain now that one day we would escape. And this day was coming soon. The next several encounters I write about are not necessarily in the order in which they actually occurred.

## Chapter Eleven

## A Glimpse of Hope

—1980—

We changed addresses many times after this. But each time we moved, our new neighbours eventually became aware of the domestic violence and alerted police. My children and I knew better than to cry for help, knowing full well it was in our best interest to remain silent. I endured the continued assaults as best I could, living in hope of the day we would escape for good.

Tom prevented us from associating with anyone and we only ventured out when absolutely necessary. My face was an open book for people to read what was happening in our lives, as more often than not, my eyes were black, front teeth chipped, my lips split and swollen. When in public, I hung my head or turned away so that if people happened to notice my injuries, I did not have to suffer their empathetic and sorrowful gazes. That is just how I felt at the time. I was filled with shame. Yet despite the police pleading with me to press charges against Tom each time they were called to our house, I refused as I became more terrified with each passing day by the very thought of the consequences this would bring upon my family, my little girls and myself. So, for the moment I could see no alternative except to stay where we were.

Tom was becoming madder than a hornet by the continued police presence at every rental home we moved to, and their desire to send him back to jail. So, he decided it best to inflict his aggression upon me *away* from wherever we happened to be residing at the time. On one occasion, he tore my upper garments clean off me as he drove, to try to prevent me from escaping. He was drinking alcohol, punching me in the side of my head and face, chain smoking and butting the cigarettes out on my legs. He continued to assault me as he drove, his aggression towards me accelerating by the minute. Then in a frenzy it seemed, he reached over and scratched my inner thighs deeply with his fingernails. My little girls remained silent in the back seat.

I cannot explain my reason for doing what I did next. As I have mentioned before, it was as though I had lost my mind. I remember we were driving in a busy part of Brisbane and there were two lanes of traffic either side of the road. I flung open the passenger door and jumped from the moving vehicle into the oncoming traffic, naked from the waist upwards, blood streaming from my face. Tom drove away with my children. I stood in the middle of the road signalling for someone to stop and help, oblivious to the state I was in. Nobody came to my aid for quite some time. Cars swerved and drove around me in fact. Finally, one of them stopped. A woman and man came running towards me with a picnic blanket, wrapped it around my half naked body, bundled me into their car and drove off. They asked me what happened, but I could not answer them as I was so distraught.

They drove me to the nearest police station. I am very vague about the series of events that followed, but I do remember not being able to make any sense to anyone for quite some time. I gathered from the questions I was being asked that the interviewing police officer assumed I had been beaten and raped. Because of the state I was in, I was escorted to another department where a detective began to question me. He became impatient when I could only express the fact that I wanted my children. He roughly pulled the blanket from my semi-naked body and when he saw the scratch marks and cigarette burns on my inner thighs, he smiled as though my injuries gave him pleasure in some sick and perverted way. He told me that he also enjoyed getting 'rough' with his wife when they came together intimately. His prying eyes made me feel like throwing up.

I cannot remember leaving the station or how I found my children and ended up back with Tom, but I do know the relief I felt when I saw that my little girls were safe and sound, seemingly unharmed physically. They explained to me how frightened they had been when I jumped from the car and said that Tom drove them to his friend's house. I could not help but notice that both of my daughters had tattoo like pictures on their legs and arms, obviously drawn using a biro. When I asked them about this, they said the kind man who owned the 'cool' house, drew on them to distract them so they would stop crying. He also gave them a tour of his home, pointing out false doors and several escape routes, explaining that this was all in place in case he had to hide from the police. I was shocked when Tom told me who the children were referring to. I had heard of this man as he was a well-known criminal. They had become friends years previous to this, whilst they both served time in prison.

In our next rental home, Tom held us captive more vigilantly than he had ever done before, and I knew he was planning to kill us. In our new location the girls were ordered to keep their bedroom windows shut and only come out of their rooms when Tom told them they could. He insisted they watch though, as he beat me, broke some of my fingers and burnt me with the butt of his cigarettes. My desire for my girls to somehow escape this situation was overwhelming now, and my every thought was consumed with the inner knowing that somehow this was going to happen. I knew only a miracle could set us free. After all, we were guarded twenty-four hours a day. We had to ask permission to move from one room of the house to another and were barricaded into our bedrooms at night. I could not bear for my children to witness any more violence and possibly my death.

My girls began to exhibit behavioural problems due to the extreme trauma they were experiencing. When Tom addressed my eldest, even if in a kindly manner, she would literally wet herself. My youngest daughter began to suffer unexplained nosebleeds, which I discovered months later were a direct result of an injury Tom had inflicted upon her in order to silence her screams the day I jumped from the car. I was so desperate to save the lives of my children, I was unafraid to give up mine, as I felt so guilty for how much they were suffering due to the poor choice I had made to be with this man. On the one hand, I knew for sure that the time of their escape was near, but a voice in my head told me different: 'You are *all* going to die'. Then we moved to another rental.

I must have had a sewing machine at some stage, because I remember making a beautiful beige velvet coat for myself out of a piece of material that had been in my possession for many years. I was secretly proud of my creation and the fact that I had made it without a pattern. This piece of fabric had miraculously managed to survive being burnt or destroyed in some other way. The day after I completed the coat, Tom ripped it to pieces in anger. I remained devoid of emotion as he threw the torn pieces of material out of the bedroom window. That same day when, I asked permission to go to the toilet, Tom sat outside the door 'guarding' it as usual. When I opened the door again, he beat me, accusing me of passing notes to the neighbours. I had never even seen our new neighbours, let alone interact with them in the way of which I was being accused.

I awoke the next morning after little sleep, expecting the day would be just like every other one had been lately, with my daughters and me living as though we were in prison. Suddenly, totally out of the blue, Tom announced he was going to the store to purchase some food. The store was less than one hundred metres from our house. He never left home without us. He threatened me as to what would happen if we tried to run, but the fact that he was going and leaving us alone surprised me. I had no intention of even attempting to escape with the girls. I was fearful this was a trick, and that he would probably wait just up the road to see what we would do.

I shook with fear when he departed, wondering what misdemeanour he would accuse me of when he returned. But then the situation seemed to turn from bad to worse when someone began banging on the front door. I was terrified, thinking our new neighbours had called the police yet again. '

'Go away and leave us alone', I called to the person on the other side of the door.

Then I heard a woman's voice pleading with me to speak to her. I could not believe that someone would have the courage to do this. I opened the door a little and told the woman to run for her life. But she stood her ground stubbornly. I explained briefly that we would all be killed, herself included, if Tom saw her anywhere near our house and suspected that she had come to try to help us in any way. The lady told me she lived next door and said she found the torn pieces of my coat in her yard. She had heard the repeated assaults and asked what she could do to help.

I felt as though I was about to throw up. I was so frightened Tom would return and discover her there. But I managed to quickly tell her that my problem was escaping with my children. Tom guarded us so vigilantly that I could see no way of us all leaving together, but could she could just help my children in some way? The lady suggested I tell the girls that the very next time Tom began to assault me, if by some miracle they had the chance, to climb out of their bedroom window. She said they should jump the fence into her yard and run into her house no matter what time of day or night, and she would protect them. I thanked her but pleaded with her to leave as Tom would surely be on his way back from the store by now. The minute she was gone I ran to the girls and told them the plan.

Two days later, the violence escalated out of control once again. It was evening and we had not long finished dinner. For the first time ever, Tom did not summon the girls to come and watch as he assaulted me. I felt joy in my heart, that no matter what happened to me now, my precious children whom I had put through so much already, would escape with the help of my kind and compassionate neighbour. She was not family or even a friend whom Tom's brothers would be likely to 'fix up', in the event of him being incarcerated, possibly for murder. I heard the bedroom window slide slowly upwards and relief flooded my heart when Tom did not appear to notice as his entire attention was on me. My precious girls were escaping to safety and they did not have to witness this final assault.

Tom smashed an empty beer bottle across the side of the dining room table and began walking slowly towards me, holding the jagged bottle threateningly in front of him. Previously he had chased me with a gun and told me how he would stab me and carve me up, but I had never been faced with a weapon such as this. He told me that this was it. He had had enough of living with such a 'low dog, slut, copper dobber,' and that he was going to 'finish me off'.

Everything seemingly went into slow motion as he walked towards me with the broken bottle. I began to retreat until I felt the cold stainless-steel edge of the kitchen sink come in contact with the small of my back and realised I was cornered. I remembered there was a carving knife in the sink that Tom had used to carve the roast for dinner that night. I knew that it was razor sharp as I had watched him sharpen it with a special stone, prior to cutting the roast. Even though I should have been terrified, I remained amazingly calm. Still facing him, I slowly reached behind me, my hand locating the knife immediately. I bought my arm back in front of me and held the knife at shoulder height with the pointed blade facing towards him.

Tom hesitated for a second, and then snarled at me: 'Come on if you are game enough. Put it here', he said, as he poked forcefully at his chest, gesturing with his forefinger to the area of his heart.

As he continued his approach, ever so slowly, I had a vision. It was as though I was watching a movie in slow motion. In the vision, I saw my daughters visiting me in prison. I had been sentenced to life for committing murder. I was appealing at the time on the grounds of self-defence and my heart was breaking because I was separated from my children. Then suddenly everything that was happening in the room came into focus once again and continued in slow motion as before. Without turning my back on Tom, I replaced the knife carefully into the sink. He was so close to me by now that I could smell alcohol on his breath as he menacingly threatened me with murder. He then took a step backwards as if to increase the momentum with which to thrust the jagged bottle into my flesh, but as he brought his arm forward, I somehow managed to duck under his raised arm and run for my life. I did not know at the time how I did this. But I now realise it could only have been by God's Grace that I managed to flee from certain death. Once outside, I jumped the neighbour's fence and ran into the safety of their home. I hugged my children with sheer and utter relief, in awe that we had all escaped.

We listened as Tom drove away from the rental home, knowing that he was searching for us, obviously oblivious that we were hiding next door. My neighbours called the police who responded immediately and drove my girls and me to a shelter in Brisbane city. I was still too afraid to press charges, so they pleaded with me to change my name, colour my hair, move overseas and wear sunglasses for the rest of my life. They warned that Tom was extremely dangerous and that I was to take his promise to kill anyone who tried to keep me from him very seriously, as they believed these were not idle threats. He had told me many times that if I ever escaped, I had better be always watching my back, because even if it took him ten years, he would eventually find and kill me. That was if his brothers had not already done so.

In the past he had sought the help of his criminal friends to track me down. On one such occasion, he arranged for two of them to pay a visit to my parents' house posing as Centrelink representatives. My mum was a very astute woman, and at first, she was highly suspicious when they arrived at her front door, briefcase in hand. After showing her fake identification and a screed of information one of them pulled from the briefcase about me, they eventually convinced her that they were in fact, who they said they were. Mum invited them into her home. She ended up making them a cup of tea and proceeded to tell them all about what had happened since I had met Tom. She explained to them that he was trying to find me and that I was in hiding with my children. One of the 'Centrelink' people said that they sympathised with her, but if she did not reveal to them my whereabouts, my payments would stop as they required a permanent address for me. It was then that my mum provided them with all the information they needed. With that, they left and gave the details they had gleaned from my unsuspecting mother, straight to Tom. No wonder the police suggested I leave the country.

## Chapter Twelve

## *Deception*

## —1980-1982—

It was hard to believe that we had finally escaped. But now my little girls and I were suffering the aftermath and were very damaged physically, mentally, emotionally and spiritually. Tom, assuming that the girls and I had fled to my parents, was now holding *them* prisoners in their own home by driving backwards and forwards, up and down their street, day and night. The only time he left them alone, was to take a brief nap here and there, and refuel his car. The police informed my poor mum and dad that they could not charge him with anything unless he actually came onto their property. I felt so sad that they were suffering also because of this situation.

The police's suggestion that we leave the country and change our identity made sense due to the psychopathic nature of the man we had managed to escape. But it just was not practical. However, the threats Tom had made kept going around and around in my mind like a broken record that would not stop. I knew that we had to hide out somewhere. I managed to find affordable accommodation in a caravan park in a secluded location at the back of the Gold Coast. The park was surrounded by beautiful farmland and natural bush and was not too far from where my parents resided at Brunswick Heads. The children began attending a small school nearby, and I, still in shock over what had taken place over the past eighteen months, did not move far from the caravan for fear that Tom may have somehow discovered our whereabouts. I felt so alone.

Early one Saturday morning, I began to think that perhaps if I could find work where I would not be exposed to the public in any way, it may help to block out the memories consuming my mind. I purchased a local newspaper from the caravan park store and scanned the 'Positions Vacant' section. One advertisement in particular caught my eye. 'Live-in Nanny' at a residence located on the canals of the Gold Coast. I would still be able to hide away, and it would be no different really from where I was living now, except that my girls and I would have our own space. It was so cramped with the three of us living in a tiny van.

I walked to the phone box at the store and dialled the number from the advertisement. A man answered and informed me that his name was Stephen (name changed for privacy reasons.) After we spoke briefly, he said he would like to meet the girls and me to further discuss the position. He went on to say he was in the process of looking to purchase a home and would like to show us a couple of properties he had in mind. This all sounded above board, so I agreed that the children and I would meet him at the front entrance to the park within the hour. As we waited, a white limousine pulled into the curb. The chauffeur opened one of the passenger doors and a man alighted and introduced himself to the girls and me as Stephen. Once inside the vehicle, I met another male passenger, who happened to be Stephen's real estate agent. As we drove, the agent told me of three homes that Stephen had recently inspected. He said his reason for accompanying us was so he could show me through each property in order that *I* could choose the one I thought would best suit the girls and me.

This seemed a little strange and I began to feel uncomfortable. I really had no clue as to what was going on, so I asked Stephen about the position and how many children would be in my care. He explained that his wife had accidentally drowned a few months previously, leaving him to look after their four-year-old daughter. He went on to say that he owned a trucking company and because he was required to be away for long periods at a time, he needed a nanny to live in. He assured me that I would rarely see him, as he was remarkably busy with his work.

After a while, we stopped in front of one of the most magnificent homes I had ever seen. The salesman showed us through this house and two others, pointing out different features in each one. All three were within walking distance of each other and equally exquisite. The agent then asked me which house I preferred. I turned to Stephen and explained that I felt it was not up to me to decide which home he was going to buy. I was so uneasy that I walked away from the two men a little so they could discuss business. From what I remember, Stephen made the final decision and arranged to meet with the agent at a later date, in order to complete the paperwork required for the sale. The agent then bid us farewell and departed in his own vehicle.

Stephen then invited the girls and me to accompany him for lunch so he could explain the finer details of the position he was offering me. We arrived in the main street of Surfers Paradise and once we began walking along the street, I could not help but notice some very unusual mannerisms this man displayed. He was immaculate in the way he dressed and wore the most expensive looking pair of shoes I had ever seen. But he had no front teeth. I wondered whether or not he had just forgotten to put them in his mouth that morning. Another thing I noticed was that every now and then while passing shop windows, he looked at his reflection and pushed his hair to the opposite side of what appeared to be his natural part. Then, as though having a mind all of its own, his hair would instantly flop back the other way. He seemed to be obsessed with fighting against it.

As we looked for a suitable place to eat lunch, we happened to come across a photo booth. This was a vending machine containing an automated coin-operated camera and film processor. Stephen insisted that my daughters and I have our photos taken. He gave us just enough coins for four snaps, specifying that he wanted a photo of me by myself, one with just the girls and two photos of the girls and me together. My daughters were thrilled with the novelty of it all, assuming that once the photos were printed, they would be theirs to keep. When we came out of the booth, Stephen asked to see the photos. After scrutinising them, he seemed satisfied by the pictures and carefully placed them in his wallet. I was a little puzzled by this, but did not really give it much thought, as I was keen to hear all about my new job.

As we proceeded further down the street, Stephen became almost manic as he continued to battle obsessively with his unruly hair. He was now hesitating at almost every second shop window, trying to pull and tame it to do something that seemed impossible. I wondered if maybe he just wanted a new look. Little did I know at this stage that that was exactly what he was trying to achieve. And for a reason I was totally unaware of. Finally, we found a restaurant which seemed to be satisfactory to this unusual man. We ordered lunch and Stephen finally discussed the position of 'live-in Nanny'.

He also enquired as to what model and make of car I liked to drive and said that he would purchase any car I wished. Once again, I became uncomfortable with his almost pushy attitude, telling him I was happy with my own car. That is when it did not break down, I thought to myself. It was such a 'bomb', but I loved it. Other than that, the position was pretty much as it was described in the advertisement. Live-in nanny with full board and a small wage. This meant that I could still hide out from Tom with the added benefit of having a large space to live in with my girls and a new little friend for them. I was very keen to meet Stephen's daughter and begin work. After lunch, the chauffeur came and drove us southward along the Gold Coast Highway to Tugun. Our destination was a nice motel, which I soon learnt had been Stephen's place of residence for the past two months.

The receptionist greeted Stephen as though he was a long-lost friend, and he asked her about the best accommodation she may have available for the next six weeks. He explained that I was going to be working for him and needed somewhere to stay with the girls whilst the sale of his house was finalised. The lady told him the penthouse was vacant for that period of time. Stephen enquired as to the price and then paid her cash. I was in awe as he handed over what looked like thousands of dollars. I began imagining what it was going to be like to spend the next six weeks with my little girls in luxury and safety. I nearly cried with sheer relief and joy. Having struggled all my life, I allowed what I thought of as a sudden stroke of good luck to totally cloud any logic or concern that this man may be up to no good. The very fact that this could be a scam and downright dangerous never entered my mind.

Stephen's rather odd appearance and the unusual behaviour he had exhibited during the last two hours or so did not alert me to anything extremely out of the ordinary. I guess considering what we had just been through this seemed as though I was being given a chance to begin a new life. All I could think of was that my girls and I could finally feel as though we were safe. We were not just some kind of gutter trash that no one really cared about. Once the accommodation arrangements were finalised, Stephen told me he would send a small truck to pick up our meagre belongings from the caravan park at nine am the next morning. He said he would arrange to have our possessions placed into storage until the sale of the house finally went through. I was to drive to the motel with the girls in my own car.

Once back at the caravan park, I decided to share this great news with my parents, almost breathless with anticipation as I imagined how excited they would be to hear the latest. Their response was the total opposite of what I had expected. I told Mum everything that had happened that day, stumbling over my words with sheer excitement. She immediately made it clear that she was genuinely concerned for our wellbeing. I tried to talk her around, to stop her being worried, but to no avail. Her words were: 'I smell a rat'. My mum told me that she and Dad would leave home in the early hours of the morning so as not to alert Tom in any way in case he followed them. They expected to arrive around seven at the caravan park. My bubble was certainly deflated, but not fully. I believed that Mum would change her mind when she witnessed the truck coming to pick up our belongings the next day and also once I showed my parents the house that the girls and I would be moving into. I could understand their concern after what we had all just been through, but this was different. Wasn't it?

My parents arrived at seven in the morning and we waited and waited and waited. The promised truck never arrived. I was devastated. I tried to phone the number that was in the paper advertising the position I had applied for but there was no answer. I could not work out how someone could do this to my little family. And why would anyone go to such lengths only to then just let us down?

I wanted to leave with my parents as they prepared to go back home that afternoon, but they were not willing to put themselves and the girls and me at risk, because Tom was still searching for us. He was still driving past their place slowly almost every day, all day, believing that my parents were harbouring my two girls and me. They kept the curtains on their sliding glass windows at the front of their home permanently closed, for fear that Tom would harm them in some way. When they left, I cried until there were no more tears. I felt empty inside. I was so lonely, especially when my girls were at school. This was an extremely hard time to go through, feeling like a total failure, yet again. Why would someone deceive me like this? What was the point in the interview, the whole day in Surfer's Paradise, the renting of the penthouse for six weeks? It made no sense to me at all.

After another month passed, I was talking to my mum on the phone one day when she mentioned that it had been over a week since Tom had stalked them. She asked whether I would like to come and stay for a couple of days. I was extremely excited at the prospect of getting out of my small habitat with the girls and spending some time away with family. My parents came and picked us up one Friday in the early hours of the morning and smuggled us into their home at Brunswick Heads. When we were on the outskirts of town, my girls and I lay on the floor and backseat of my father's car, just in case Tom was around. We left the curtains drawn as a precautionary measure for the entire time we visited.

On Sunday morning, I woke to the sound of my mother in the kitchen making a pot of tea. I loved to spend time with her and Dad, chatting and catching up, so I joined her. My dad and the girls were still asleep, so Mum and I made the most of our time together. I did not have much to contribute in the way of news, as all I had been doing was hiding out in a caravan all day every day. While we were talking, I happened to glance at the Sunday paper lying on the table. There on the very front page was a photo of Stephen. I told Mum that this was the man who had offered me the position on the Gold Coast. It was obvious to me that she had read the article prior to me waking, not only by the horrified look on her face, but by the urgency with which she went and woke my father, asking him to dress quickly and drive me to the local police station.

In the meantime, I scanned the article. I was horrified to discover that this man's name was not Stephen at all, and that he was in fact a previous business partner of another man in a corporation that had gone bust. Stephen was the co-founder of this corporation and had disappeared in June 1980, around the time his partner in business was found deceased in his vehicle, with a .30-calibre rifle beside him. It was presumed at the time that he had committed suicide. Corporate and police investigators, ASIO, and the FBI had started to investigate the joint company. I was in a state of shock.

Once we arrived at the police station, I was ushered into an interview room and asked about my association with Stephen. I relayed the whole story about how I had simply answered an advertisement for a live-in nanny position and the events that had followed. The police then told me that the receptionist from the motel where Stephen was staying had been to see them. She informed them that not long after the children and I left her motel that day, Stephen returned to his room briefly, then came back downstairs saying that he was going for a walk. But he did not return and that was the last time she saw him. He left money, house plans and clothing in the room. The real estate agent had also come forward after reading the newspaper article and Stephen had actually purchased the property from him.

When I told the police about the photo booth and the photos Stephen had so specifically ordered of my daughters and me, one of the interviewing detectives explained that it was more than likely he would have already used the photos to help change his identity and to make it look as though we were his wife and children. After this, I did not hear anything much about Stephen except that he was missing, and that possibly he had been murdered. Then in 1982 I read in the newspaper of someone sighting him in Thailand. Now and again over the next few years I noticed an article here and there about him and other possible sightings, but nothing eventuated. In 2015, thirty-five years after my encounter with this man, my oldest daughter, who was nine years old at the time we met Stephen, phoned me urging me to watch the program 60 Minutes, as he had been located.

I was in shock as the reporter shared how they had found Stephen, now aged 73, in a small town in America. He had been missing, presumed dead, for 35 years. An Australian author from Sydney had followed up on Stephen himself, had somehow found him and then contacted 60 Minutes. I wondered how an author from Australia could find and expose one of Australia's most wanted fugitives, when supposedly both American and Australian authorities had failed to. By the time 60 Minutes caught up with him, he was operating his own business, manufacturing tactical weapons for US and Special Forces, groups, hunters, and special operations.

Stephen to my knowledge, has never been convicted, even though he ripped off many people through the company he co-owned with his business partner. A Royal Commission found evidence of a false passport and false declarations to customs, clandestine intelligence activities, drug-dealing, gun-running and organised crime. And these are just a few of the illegal activities this man has been involved in. Stephen left Australia illegally in 1980, not long after my association with him.

It was after this latest disaster I had innocently gotten my children and myself involved in, that my mum insisted that I write my story. She said, 'Only you could manage to get yourself mixed up in something such as this'. I wondered at the time why she would say that?

## Chapter Thirteen

## The Power of Forgiveness

### —1982-1983—

My tiny abode was beginning to feel like a jail cell. Once the girls left for school in the morning and I had nothing else to distract me, my mind became my worst enemy. Guilt and shame over my crazy decision to form a relationship with my previous partner and the impact this had had on my children and family hung over me like a storm cloud. Plus, the degree of pain and loss I still felt for my son, even though it had been ten years since his birth. I began to wonder if things could get any worse.

One day, the driving desire to find him tormented me so much that I decided to register with a support group for adoptees. I was living in hope that my son's adoptive parents may also register in order to gain more information about my family history. I was desperate to communicate with them. I would have especially loved to have photos and to know if he was healthy and strong. Did he enjoy school? What were his hobbies and interests? Was he 'sport mad' as I had been at the same age? Did he have siblings? Was he quiet or outgoing? And so forth... I yearned to know all about him. And should his parents not wish to seek me out, my name would at least be on the register so he could contact me when he was older, if he so desired. I also registered with a group called 'Jigsaw', an association that provided support for those affected in any way by the adoption process. In particular, they assisted birth mothers, fathers and adopted adults and their families, who may need help due to the process of forced adoption.

My parents were still reluctant for my children and me to visit them, except for on the odd occasion. If Tom discovered we were in the vicinity, it would place all of our lives at risk and the game of cat and mouse would begin all over again. Recently, they had had enough stress of their own to deal with. Not only was my mum not well, she was also trying to cope with Dad who was beginning to experience short-term memory loss.

Out of sheer desperation I reached out to my sister-in-law, via a phone call. She listened in disbelief as I recounted the story of the events that had occurred over the past two years and explained the reason why it was unsafe for us to seek refuge at my parents' house. Despite this, she insisted that the girls and I come and stay with her until we could find a secure place to live. I was so grateful, but not wanting to put her life in danger, I began searching for work as soon as we arrived at her home. I discovered another 'live-in nanny' advertisement in the local newspaper and made contact by phone. I was fortunate to speak to the lady who was temporarily filling this position. She told me the job involved taking care of three young children while their father was at work. The children's mother had passed away suddenly only a couple of months previously. The lady knew the family well and was helping out until a suitable nanny could be found. She told me how lovely and respectful the father of the children was and assured me that she would pass my details on to him.

Two days later he phoned me and arranged to meet in order to discuss the position. I listened intently as he explained exactly what he expected of the person he was seeking. He told me the children were grieving for their mother and how difficult he was finding this. He was also was attempting to come to grips with the sudden loss of his wife. I had decided ahead of time to be totally honest about how the girls and I had been hiding out from Tom and the circumstances surrounding our situation. In spite of this, he asked me if I would accept the position and told me he would protect my children and me as best he could, should the need arise. The girls and I moved to his home the next day. I loved caring for the three children and did my best to comfort them. My daughters and I began to relax a little, feeling less frightened as each day passed. But our glimpse of living a normal life was short-lived. After six months or so, my employer met a lady who had six children. They fell in love and as their relationship developed, I realised that it was time for us to leave.

Since almost a year had passed with no sign of Tom, I assumed it was safe for us to finally live by ourselves. But I still remained on the lookout, as the fear of him somehow finding us, or harming my family, lingered for at least the next ten years. I found a flat in a tumbledown old block of units situated in a beachside suburb of the city. There was a hotel across the road, so once we had settled in, I enquired to see if there were any positions vacant. It so happened that the publican was about to advertise for a bar attendant, so I began work the very next week. After I had been employed at the hotel for a month or so, one of the regular customers asked me on a date and not long after, we decided to move in together. I became pregnant and my third daughter was born on September 24th, 1982. Labour began at approximately 2.30am, and due to the frequency and intensity of the contractions from their onset, I thought it best to phone the hospital to let them know of my impending arrival. The midwife I spoke to was very reassuring and said she looked forward to seeing me. She asked if I had delivered any other children at that hospital so she could retrieve my medical record in preparation for my arrival. I told her about my son who had been born there in 1970.

On arrival, I gingerly walked through the sliding glass doors into the maternity section of the hospital, feeling as though my baby was going to enter the world at any moment. The midwife greeted me and asked if I remembered her. With one thing only on my mind, I requested to be taken to the labour ward so that I could get on with the business of delivering my baby. My beautiful little girl entered the world soon after. It was when she was taken away to have the routine Apgar score test that the midwife asked me once again. 'Do you remember me'?

'No, I replied'. I looked at her more carefully now, as my body was no longer wracked with the pain of childbirth, and I could concentrate. I noticed she had tears in her eyes.

She had been very compassionate and encouraging during the delivery of my baby, but now she appeared to be deeply troubled. It was then she hesitantly revealed to me how she had read my medical records as I was on route to the hospital and discovered that she had been with me when I was in labour with my son. She recalled the dreadful way she had treated me twelve years previously. Tears now stained her face as she begged me to forgive her. She told me that the nursing staff and midwives were instructed by the matron of the hospital back in those days to treat unmarried mothers with utter disdain. Supposedly, this was for the birth mother's own good; to be a lesson to them not to fall pregnant again prior to marriage. I listened intently as she explained this to me and I became aware for the very first time that I had given a family who could not have children of their own, the gift of a beautiful child. Suddenly I was no longer angry or hurt by the injustice of my baby being taken from me, even though I still grieved for him.

I remembered what I had learned as a young child growing up in church, of the absolute necessity to forgive others for past hurts and how un-forgiveness actually keeps us a prisoner of Satan. I looked at the beautiful lady standing before me and recognised that she was very sincere in wanting this great burden of guilt she had carried for the past twelve years removed from her life. It was easy to forgive her now that I understood why she had treated me in the manner she had. We held each other and cried tears of joy, as the burdens of what we had each carried, lifted from us. Oh, the power of forgiveness.

When I returned home with our new addition to the family, I was greeted by two excited girls, who were now ten and eleven years old. They were very willing helpers as we settled into a new routine, making allowance for this precious little one. But my partner whom I will call John, began to act differently. Sometimes just out of the blue, he would stop talking to me. The silence between us would often last up to four days or more. Because I always assumed responsibility for the way people responded to me, I tried to recall each conversation, searching my mind for clues about what *I* had said or done that may have upset him. It was as though I was back in my first marriage, not knowing how to communicate and speak my feelings. Because I did not know how to express myself, let alone feel worthy enough to do so, I became resentful and angry deep within, whilst wearing a mask of happiness as though I had not a care in the world. I thought I was the only one suffering in silence, but little did I realise that John was, also. He had been in the army long before I met him and fought on the front line during the Vietnam War. Alcohol had become his best friend, so he could temporarily blot out the memories of the horrific atrocities he obviously had witnessed.

I now realise that we were two very broken people who were expecting one another to somehow fill the emptiness we both felt within. Neither realised that it is not possible to replace or fix anything lacking in another, let alone change the way they are. While he sought solace through alcohol, I began searching for answers to the meaning of life, hoping when I found them it would change not only me, but the lives of my entire family. I heard about an association called Ekankar and made contact. I was assured by some of the members that if I studied and observed the spiritual practices of the sect, I would experience a personal connection with God. I drank in the contents of the books I was given, falsely believing a lie that I had finally found what I so desperately sought. I even taught my older daughters the basic principles, so they also could discover how to live a good and fruitful life.

John's addiction to alcohol put pressure on us financially, which meant there was little money to purchase food and other necessities. Our relationship deteriorated even more so, as we struggled to make ends meet. He was unemployed at the time and as much as I hate to admit this, I became exceptionally good at stealing from him, in order for us to survive. In those desperate times, I would wait until he fell into a deep sleep on the floor in front of the television, then carefully remove his wallet from his back pocket, taking just enough money to purchase groceries or other necessities. Strangely enough, he never realised money was missing from his wallet.

I am not sure what came over him, but one day he decided he had better look for work. It was not long before he was offered a job in a small town, approximately a three-hour drive from where we lived. The work was permanent, so we decided to pack up and move to a caravan park in the area. My two older daughters took a short cut to school each day through a dairy farm, purchasing fresh milk for us in the afternoon on their way home. While the relationship between John and me was not improving, my children and friends kept me going. As a family, we were often invited to attend barbecues in the pine forest next to the park and other social family outings. About once a month, I packed the children and some luggage in the car and drove to my parents' house in New South Wales to spend a few days with them. These small distractions helped a little to keep my mind from dwelling too much on the past.

## Chapter Fourteen

## Alternative Lifestyle

## —1983-1985—

Now that John had full time employment, we decided to place a deposit on a ten-acre block of land located twenty kilometres from his work. Although the block was mainly scrub, we enjoyed spending time there on his days off. We cleared a space for a small camping area and hired a contractor to make a dam at the base of a steep slope, approximately thirty metres from the main area. John managed to obtain a few large timber boxes from his work, which had been used to transport huge machinery and other equipment. Some were large enough for us to utilise as a temporary dwelling. One box became our kitchen, another a bedroom and the third smaller box we made into our bathroom. We then purchased a second-hand caravan for the girls to use as their bedroom.

John cut windows in each box, placed hinges on the cut-out pieces and attached them to the openings. We used second-hand corrugated iron to make a roof and purchased guttering and a couple of rainwater tanks. The local sawmill had long off-cuts of bark on their throw-away pile, so we brought trailer loads of these back to the block and nailed them to the outside of the wooden boxes. Our dwelling then resembled a snug log cabin. We were fortunate enough to find an old-fashioned claw foot bath, bush-shower, copper, kerosene fridge and a wood stove at a farm sale in our local area. The latter three items were absolutely essential, as we had no power to the block. When all was completed, we towed our mobile home from the caravan park and moved to our block permanently. My older girls travelled via a minibus to school, the eldest remaining at the same high school she had been attending prior to our move; her younger sister changing to a small primary school not more than five kilometres from home. It was now approximately May 1983.

To begin with, living in the bush was a real novelty. But after six months or so of trying to clear the seemingly never ending lantana bushes close to our dwelling and doing without the luxury of plumbing and power, I began to feel as though I was a pioneer from the 1800's. Winter was bitterly cold and even with the wood stove burning, it offered little comfort as the wind whipped through every crevice of our box house. Eventually we purchased a generator but only used it at night for light and to run the washing machine on the weekend.

With our dam now full to the brim, I pleaded with John to install a pump in order to bring water to our dwelling. But nothing ever eventuated. I don't think he realised how hard it was for me to carry full buckets from the dam up the steep slope to our living area each day. I made many trips up and down that slope, rain, hail, or shine. Water was required to fill the copper for baths and showers, wash our clothes and to service a large vegetable garden I had made. I became very fit, but the problem was that I was losing weight rapidly. It became very obvious just how hard it was living in the bush, when we visited friends or family who, of course, had all the normal facilities we so obviously lacked.

With the extra burden of large repayments for our block of land, the cost of the generator, chainsaws, fencing and specialised household items that did not require electricity, there was little left over from my partner's pay each week., I realised that the best way for us to survive was to be as self-sufficient as possible. We purchased some milking goats, one black sheep, chickens, turkeys, geese and ducks. It took the children a little while to adjust to the strong flavour of milk from the goats, but once they did, they actually preferred it to cows' milk. Even though I no longer suffered with bulimia, I was still obsessed with healthy eating. I loved the fact that we were able to consume the fresh and healthy food we produced ourselves.

I used the eggs from the geese, chickens and ducks to bake biscuits, healthy snacks, omelettes and quiches, and made cheese from the goat's milk. The only food items we purchased were sugar, flour, and food for the animals. I was an avid reader of 'Grass Roots' magazine and obtained many tips about how to create anything; whether a structure or food product, from whatever was readily available in our own garden or the immediate surroundings. I began to make mud bricks down by the dam, dreaming of the day I would have enough to make a dwelling for us. The vegetable garden thrived and although there was no threat from insects, I did have another predator who was relentless in her efforts to consume its contents. It was my favourite milking goat I called 'Nanny'. She tried everything she could to break through the fence in order to sample the contents of the garden. Her fruitless attempts made me laugh. We could have eaten goat meat as well, but due to my second daughter's severe illness when she was eighteen months old, the children and I consumed mainly a vegetarian diet.

I adored my small goat herd. As I milked them each afternoon, I was reminded of the dairy cows on the family farm where I grew up. One day a man called by to see if I would like another nanny goat. She was pregnant, and I couldn't resist her. I named her Snowflake. But we soon discovered that Snowflake did not have a very nice attitude towards people. In fact, she didn't like anyone or anything for that matter, except for me. I kept her on a chain for the first little while until she got used to her new environment. John attempted to make friends with her one night when he had been drinking, but she wanted nothing to do with him. Eventually he annoyed her so much, that she somehow wound herself around his legs with her chain, causing him to fall to the ground. I heard his desperate cries for help, and when I came to his rescue and realised what had happened, I almost laughed despite the seriousness of the situation. There was Snowflake standing over him with her forehead almost touching his, staring him straight in the eye. It was as though she was warning him to never tease her again.

My children loved the animals but were saddened by the fact that Snowflake didn't feel the same way towards them. My second eldest daughter tried everything to make this angry goat like her. I suggested that she give her a treat, thinking that this may just work. So, she went to the cabin to get some fruit, but unbeknown to me, Snowflake had followed her inside. Before long I heard a shrill scream, then watched in horror as my daughter fled from the cabin, fruit in hand, with Snowflake's head level with her little behind, ready to bunt her. After this episode, the girls avoided that intolerant goat as best they could. Snowflake gave birth to twins around the time my baby girl had just started to walk. When the goat 'kids' were only a few weeks old, they decided to make friends with my baby, unintentionally hurting her by knocking her to the ground. I had no choice but to give them away.

The very next day, I was walking between our box house and the chook pen to feed the chickens and collect the eggs. My mother-in-law was visiting at the time and was following along behind me with my little girl. Suddenly, Snowflake came from behind our car and bunted my baby in the forehead. I heard her scream and rushed to pick her up. As I lay her back on my arm to inspect the damage, I saw blood already pooling into her eye socket from a deep gash. I thought Snowflake may have possibly taken her eye as well. I ran with her to the cabin to get something to stem the bleeding. Without investigating further, I placed a cloth nappy over her forehead, handed her to my mother-in-law and drove us speedily to the closest medical centre. The doctor peeled away the nappy, now soaked with blood and to my sheer relief, my little one's eye was unaffected. She had a deep gash to her forehead that required six stitches. Once home again, I found a new owner for Snowflake as I knew what her fate would be if she was still at our block when John returned from work.

Meanwhile, we purchased a pony for the children called Tiny. One day when my eldest daughter climbed onto his back, he tried every which way he could to get her off. When he realised she wasn't letting go, he took off at full speed. Fearing the worst, I jumped into the car and drove up the road a few kilometres to where I knew there was a fence. I could hear my daughter's frantic screams as Tiny raced with her on his back, through the bush. Next thing I knew, he came galloping towards the fence, stopped suddenly sending my daughter hurtling through the air onto the other side. Luckily, she was uninjured.

Once the girls left for school each day and my little one was taking her morning nap, I ventured into the bush to gather kindling for the wood stove and copper. A man and his wife, whom John had become acquainted with through his work, often visited and helped me with the supply of larger firewood. They chain-sawed dead timber on our block into rounds for me. I became an expert at splitting the rounds with an axe into smaller, more manageable size pieces to fit the firebox of the wood stove. In the winter months, as I searched for kindling, I often noticed little woolly jumpers and cardigans I had put on my goats to keep them warm caught up on bushes and low hanging branches. I chuckled to myself as I imagined them standing on their hind legs in order to consume fresh leaves that were higher up than they could reach normally, causing their woollen garments to catch on whatever they came in contact with, on their descent.

One day whilst sitting beside the dam, Tiny came to quench his thirst. I observed him closely, in awe of his beauty as the rays of light from the sun, filtered through the trees causing his sleek coat to glisten as he drank thirstily. Suddenly he turned as though startled and looked at me. It was as though he knew what I was thinking about him. He came and nudged me lovingly. I was astounded. I had had similar experiences with my goats. When this first began happening, I thought nothing of it. But then, I became obsessed with my discovery and began to experiment, using my mind to make each animal, one by one, turn and look at me. All I did was gaze at them with love filling my heart.

On another occasion as I sat meditating beside the dam, I felt a gentle 'tugging' on my hair. I remained very still, as I realised it was a small bird. It tugged and pulled some hair from my head, then flew to a tree. Back it came again and again, each time fearlessly pulling stands of hair from my head. I realised as months went by that I had a very special connection with animals and birds. They were totally unafraid of me. This became commonplace with wild birds coming and sitting on my head, while I sat alone at the dam. Years later I had a similar experience. On this particular occasion, I was on a beach lying face down on my towel on the sand, reading a book, when I noticed a large shadow fall across the pages. Before I could react, I felt scratching and pulling of my hair. I scrambled to my feet with fright and saw a huge eagle hovering above me. It was almost as though it had been trying to pick me up by the hair. It was a rather painful experience, due to its talons, scratching my scalp. When I told one of my friends, she laughed and said that she could understand the reason birds were attracted to my hair, as it is very thick and coarse. I guess it would be ideal to contribute as part of the building material, for birds making their nests.

Other strange things happened, as well. One day when my baby girl was sleeping and the older girls were at school, I decided to try to connect with God by meditating once again. That is, to connect with the person I perceived God to be, through my study of the *Ekankar* book I had been given. I assumed that if I could connect with Him, He may somehow teach me how to have a normal relationship with my partner – and that by some miraculous revelation, I might discover a way to change myself, and who I was. I began by clearing my mind of all thoughts. The next minute, it was as though I was being transported out of my body and into space. I travelled quickly and then 'landed' somewhere out there. Everything looked so different. There were flowerbeds full of fragrant blossoms more colourful than any I had ever seen before. I began walking along a narrow pathway, which led to a church-like structure with a grand wooden door. As I placed my hand on the large brass doorknob, the door opened of its own accord. I peered hesitantly inside and saw a staircase leading down into what looked like an amphitheatre. Candles on both sides of the stairs lit the way as I walked towards a large stage. At the foot of the stairs was an enormous glowing light. A conversation began to take place between this 'light' and myself. Then sheer terror came upon me, causing me to come back into my body with a thud. I cannot recall one word of that conversation.

On this particular occasion, I believe I astral travelled in the same way I had as a small child. I now realise that because I was delving into practices of the occult unknowingly, assuming that I was seeking God, I was actually being deceived by Satan. Satan comes as a counterfeit to kill, steal and destroy and to deceive the world into following his evil practices and ways. I believe I was receiving information from the spirit world, but I was tuning in to the wrong channel. I was receiving sound waves and information from Satan's network. Instead of becoming still before the Lord and waiting on Him, I was unknowingly becoming still before Satan and was being used as an instrument by the very enemy of God.

We met some very unusual characters whilst living on our block. One of these was a man who loved to cook and insisted on sharing his 'delicacies' with others. One day we visited his house to check on him, as we had heard from other townsfolk that he had been quite ill. When we arrived, he invited us in, assuring us that he had fully recovered from his ailment. I noticed a big pot of stew simmering gently on his old rusted-out combustion stove. A tea towel was hanging loosely over the top of the pot, and judging by its appearance, it was way past its useful days, offering little protection to the stew within, as blowflies swarmed in a frenzy above. I asked the man what he was cooking and mistakenly remarked about how good it smelled. With that, he lifted the 'holey' protective covering, stepping aside as one hundred or so flies made their escape from the kangaroo tail stew he proudly showed me.

The very next evening, the man arrived at our block with a big pot which I recognised immediately, as the one from the day before. He announced that seeing as I loved the smell of his stew, he had decided to share it with us for dinner. Thank goodness I had an excuse. A 'vegetarian' excuse. I felt sick to the pit of my stomach. All I could think of was that swarm of flies I had witnessed the previous day escaping from under the hole-ridden tea towel. I could barely eat my salad as I prayed a silent prayer of protection for the safety and wellbeing of my children and John, as I watched them consume the stew and return to the pot for second helpings.

On another occasion, the same man purchased a live rooster. He placed it on the back seat of his car, wound the windows up so it could not escape, and feeling rather thirsty, he decided to stop at the local pub on his way home, to down an ale or two. It was the middle of summer, so as you can imagine, the poor rooster was long dead and possibly half roasted, by the time he came out of the pub. Having no regard for the way the poor fowl had died, he took it home, plucked it, cooked it and ate it for his dinner.

As time went on, life on our block became more difficult for me. The kindling from the area immediately surrounding the cabin was dwindling, which meant I had to venture even further into the bush to restock my supply. As the vegetable garden increased in size and rendered more produce, more water from the dam was required. This meant more trips up and down the hill, carrying countless buckets each day. Sometimes I felt as if my arms were almost dragging on the ground, as I lumped the full buckets up the hill to the living area. As I went about my chores, I had a lot of time to think about my past and also how unhappy I was feeling about the present situation I was in. And I was still grieving the loss of my son, even though I loved my girls with all my heart.

The friends who helped me with the firewood supply seemed to sense my sad demeanour, despite the fact that I attempted to hide my true feelings. On more than one occasion they offered me some marijuana, assuring me that it would make me feel better. I refused their offers, until one day when they visited, I was feeling so low that I decided to try a little. My older girls were at school and only my baby and I were home. I had two drags and don't remember much more about the afternoon. My friends told me later that they put me to bed with my toddler. Apparently, I could not even walk. I felt so ashamed of myself.

On another occasion when these same friends came to chainsaw trees for me into rounds while my partner was at work, they discovered my three daughters and me so ill with gastro and vomiting, that we could not even get out of our beds. Somehow, they managed to get us all into their car and took us to the doctor. My doctor was aware of the hardship I endured on the block and the physical toll this lifestyle was having on my body. He weighed me, stating I was severely underweight and that if I did not take his advice and stop living the way I was, he was afraid I may die. I took him seriously and the girls and I moved to Brisbane to live with my mother-in-law. John remained on the block, visiting us most weekends.

## Chapter Fifteen

## City Life

## —1985 to 1988—

After relocating, it took a little while to adjust to the routine of city living. Even though we now had the luxury of electricity and running water, I missed the alternate lifestyle and the peace and quiet of the bush. I felt for my older girls, as once again they had to say goodbye to their friends, attend a new school and begin all over again. They were now in year eight and nine, respectively.

I loved living with my mother-in-law and recognised how hard it must be for her to suddenly have another adult and three children in her home after living alone for many years. She encouraged me to seek work, offering to take care of my four-year-old daughter. She had a wicked sense of humour, but at the same time, was one of the most gracious and patient ladies you could ever meet. Nothing was ever too much trouble for her. Even though my older two daughters were from my first marriage, she accepted them as her own grandchildren, often playing board games with them for hours at a time. They loved her dearly.

After a month or so, I found work at a large fruit and vegetable processing plant. I left my four-year-old little girl in the care of her grandmother, feeling fortunate to have such a trustworthy and kind babysitter. I soon discovered that there was a variety of tasks within this huge factory, all performed at the same time in different sections. Some of these tasks involved canning, preserving, packing, sorting, grading, peeling, and slicing the fruit. My first experience within the factory was working on the pineapple line. Our job was to peel the pines in preparation for them to be sliced and placed into cans. There were four of us on each line. Every day, I worked with the same three women, who had been employed at the cannery for many years and were very experienced at the job. These ladies and I stood beside the conveyer belt, and as the pineapples came past us at intervals in groups of four, we were each expected to pick up a pine, regardless of whether we had finished peeling the previous one or not. We placed the unpeeled pineapples onto a cutting board beside us, and more often than not, my pile on the board was so high that they would sometimes tumble onto the floor. I always managed to peel each one, though, catching up to the other women when there was a break in the line.

Before long, I noticed that my co-workers seemed to have time to chat with one another between peeling. That was, unless a supervisor happened to be in the vicinity. When this was the case, they would end up in the same predicament as me, with pines stacking up and falling on the floor. I decided to observe how they managed to peel their pines so quickly when not under the watchful eye of the hierarchy, and to hopefully learn some tips on becoming faster at the job. I could hardly believe my eyes when I learned their secret. They hacked into each pine, removing the skin and most of the flesh with it, tossing the skin into the bin along with most of the pineapple. I did not follow suit.

At times I was required to help out in other areas of the factory. I made friends very easily, mostly with ladies who were quite a bit older than me. One day, I happened to be working alongside one of my new friends, placing empty cans onto trays, then feeding them on to a conveyor belt. It was such a monotonous job and before long, I began to think about my little herd of milking goats, Tiny the pony and the other animals and birds on our bush block. I thought about the way in which I could make them turn and look at me when I focused on them for long enough.

I decided to see if this same technique would work with humans and began to focus on a few people, one by one, who were within my line of vision. Each time without fail, they turned and looked straight at me, seemingly confused as to why they had actually done so. Over the tremendous din of the clanging and banging of cans and other factory noise, I managed to tell my friend what I had just experienced, through the power of the human mind. I got the distinct feeling she was not happy about what I had revealed to her, even though she looked a little puzzled about how I thought I could possibly do this. So, in order to prove this phenomenon to her, I pointed out one of the foremen who was supervising a job quite a distance from us and began to focus on him, willing him in my mind to turn and look at me. After a few minutes, he spun around, looking straight past at least another forty or more factory workers, obviously focusing his attention on me. My co-worker was aghast and told me we needed to discuss what had just taken place, in our next break.

Later, as we sat together in the lunchroom, she took out her Bible and showed me certain scriptures, explaining that what I had just shown her within the factory was evil. It was, in fact, demonic. She agreed that I had definitely used some sort of 'power' to do these things, but it was not right in God's eyes. I took what she said very seriously. Even though I had walked away from the Church when I was a teenager, I had never walked away from God. I was, in fact, still searching for Him. That is why I had been involved in Eckankar. I was desperate to find Him.

I had only been employed at the factory for a few months when one of the supervisors asked if I would be interested in becoming a hostess. This involved showing tourists through the plant and explaining the different processes that were taking place. I jumped at the chance, as I saw this offer as a great opportunity to give me a break from the monotony of the factory work. I was excited and could not wait to tell my friends.

As things turned out, they definitely were not as excited as I was and did not attempt in any way to hide their jealousy. I did not realise until they explained to me that they had never been given this same opportunity, despite the fact most of them had worked in the factory for years. When I approached these ladies in the lunchroom the next day, no one spoke to me despite my attempts to converse with them. It reminded me of a school yard tiff, when children use silence as a weapon to ostracise someone from their group. I got the message loud and clear and after a couple of months I quit working at the factory. It was not long before I began another job, cleaning offices in a high-rise building in the city. I travelled by train from the suburb where we lived, leaving home around four o'clock each afternoon. I began work at five thirty, cleaned three floors of the building in three hours, then caught the train back home again.

The relationship between John and me seemed to improve now that we only saw each other on weekends. There were actually some really nice times, which made life a lot easier for the children. Then one day he proposed to me and I accepted. It was as though I got carried away by the moment and the whole idea of us becoming one big happy family. My gorgeous mother-in-law and other female relatives set about planning menus, venues and so on. Before I could barely blink, there I was walking towards him down a red carpet in his cousin's back yard, about to make what should have been one of the biggest commitments of my life.

After we married, things were fine for a little while, then everything went back to how it had been before. Nothing had really changed as had I hoped it would, and once again, we grew further and further apart. There are always two sides to a story, though. This was not only John's fault. I did not know how to communicate and tell him how sad I was feeling about the way he seemed to put alcohol before his little family. He was offered work in a smaller town five hours from the city, so we moved once again. It was now 1986.

My daughters and I had family from my first marriage who had lived in the area for many years, so I contacted them when we arrived. 'Aunty,' as I affectionately called her, and most of her nine children and my three daughters and I would often go fishing once school was over for the day. It was so much fun as we sat on the riverbank, sometimes for hours at a time, fishing and watching the children play, often returning home with enough fish for dinner. At other times just Aunty and I would fish all day. This entire family played a huge part in our lives while we resided in this coastal town and still do to this day.

However, once again money became very tight, so I decided to look for employment. I thought all my dreams had come true when I noticed a position advertised in the local paper for a childcare worker in a women's refuge. Despite the fact that the advertisement clearly stated that the main specification for the job was that the person had to be qualified in this field of work, I applied anyway. I had almost forgotten about my application, when I received a phone call a few weeks later, asking me to attend an interview. I must admit that is when I began to doubt that I would have any chance of securing this position. But ever since the girls and I had been taken to refuges and had received so much encouragement, love, and support, I had had a passion to help abused women and children.

When I sat before a panel of four during the interview, they seemed as baffled as I was, as to why I had even bothered to apply for this position, since I had none of the required criteria for the job. I was wondering why they had called me for an interview when they told me that many with the required qualifications had applied for the same position. Once I realised that I had nothing to lose and probably had no chance of being employed by this association anyway, I was incredibly open and honest with the panel, telling them a little of my story. I revealed that my daughters and I had been in women's shelters several times and that both while we were in the safety of the shelters and since we had been free from domestic violence, I had a burning desire to find employment in this line of work. I walked away from the interview and basically forgot all about it. I was shocked when I received a phone call a fortnight later, inviting me to come for a second interview. At this particular meeting with the panel, they asked only a couple more questions and then informed me that they had decided to employ me for the position. Once again, it was as though they were as puzzled as I was by their decision.

I was employed as a childcare worker and night supervisor when required. What I enjoyed most about my job was interacting with the children, loving and caring for them while their mum's attended court proceedings or solicitors appointments etc., as part of the process of moving on from the violence and abuse that had bought them to the shelter in the first place. I did my best to distract the children, if only temporarily, from the sadness and trauma that most of them had experienced. It reminded me of what my girls had been through with Tom. I also loved spending time with the Mums when I was on night supervisor duty and their little ones were tucked up safely in their beds. I considered myself as no more than a listening ear for them as they poured out their hearts to me. I had no counselling qualifications, so I just listened as they told me what they had been through. I did not share my story, but I think some of them guessed that maybe I had been in a similar situation, due to my genuine compassion, love, acceptance and understanding towards them.

Even though I now had an income, it was not enough to make ends meet. John was in and out of work, so the money I earned from the shelter did not go far. We seemed to be living from week to week with no savings for emergencies, and that worried me, so I applied for a job in a hotel as a bar attendant. This job involved night work, which meant I could work at the shelter during the day, go home for a quick shower, and be back at the hotel in time to work the night shift. The boss at my second job allocated me work in a bar which was a little 'classier' than a public bar, but in reality, it was not really that much better. More often than not, alcohol-fuelled brawls broke out between some of the patrons, causing me to have flash backs to my relationship with Tom. I found myself cowering beside the bar whenever this happened, and once my shift was over and I was back in the safety of my home, I experienced nightmares about what the girls and I had suffered.

With the pressures of the extra job, I felt exhausted and an emotional wreck. My search for God through Eckankar, did not seem to be producing any results and my mind was still my worst enemy. So, in my desperate search for some kind of help and to find the peace and happiness I so desperately yearned for, I decided to join the Hare Krishna movement. I began meeting with the Krishnas and rising at three o'clock each morning, to chant the Krishna mantra. However, despite the lovely friends I made, I still felt empty. I began attending different churches, expecting to feel instantly happy and fulfilled on the very first visit, and when that did not happen, I drifted to another, the very next Sunday.

Then it was as though my security blanket was ripped from beneath me, when my ex-husband's Aunty, Uncle and family, relocated to

Western Australia. It was so hard to say goodbye to them, as they had been our best friends for some time, and Aunty had been my saving grace by distracting me from my circumstances now and then. One day not long after they had left, I came to the point where I could not take any more stress and had to do something about it. John was still drinking excessively, and I was exhausted from trying to work two jobs, plus deal with everything else that seemed to be going wrong in our lives. I packed some clothes, took the children and rented a caravan near the beach. Due to the state I was in, I could not possibly continue to work, so I quit both jobs and went to Centrelink to apply for financial assistance.

The girls and I survived on benefits, even having enough money left at the end of each week to purchase a few treats after paying rent and buying food and other necessities. I could not believe it. I did not have to work two jobs and be resentful anymore and no longer needed to steal from my husband and feel ashamed of myself for doing so. It was as though a big weight had been lifted from my shoulders for the first time in years.

But I began to feel nauseous and after a week or so, the realisation hit me that I was pregnant. I put off telling John until I was about two months along the way. When I finally told him, he was extremely excited thinking that this meant we would 'have to' get back together. I was willing to raise this little one and my other children by myself, as it was so peaceful and easy with just us girls. But as time went on, my husband made a lot of promises to me, so I decided to give our marriage another try.

A few weeks later my ex-husband's family contacted us and said there was work available in Western Australia, if we were willing to relocate. They offered John a room in their home until such time as the girls and I could join him. He jumped at the chance, booked himself an airfare and was gone within a couple of weeks. This left my girls and me to sort out yet another rental home full of furniture. But this time, instead of needing to care for a new baby as I packed, I suffered from extreme morning sickness. Another worry presented itself also. My eldest daughter was in year eleven and was not keen to leave and come with us. I did not blame her due to the emotional upheavals my children had endured, as I randomly moved them from one relationship to another and place to place. The mother of a girlfriend of hers, offered for her to board at their home so that she could stay and at least finish the school year.

After I finished packing up the house, my two younger daughters and I moved in with my parents in northern New South Wales and waited for our air tickets to arrive. Time went by, and finally, my husband told me that he could not afford for us to fly and instead had booked us on a bus. The trip took five days and I was extremely uncomfortable as I was now seven months pregnant. For the first day and night, I tried desperately to stay awake as I was concerned that I might accidentally go to sleep on the shoulder of the young man sitting next to me. As you can imagine by the second evening, I was exhausted and slept like a baby, unwittingly using the young man's shoulder as a pillow. I woke at daybreak feeling happy at first that I had had such an amazing rest, until I realised my concern had become a reality. It was very embarrassing for both him and me.

By the time we arrived at our destination, my feet and legs were so swollen that the driver had to carry me down the stairs of the bus. After a couple of days, everything seemed to have settled back to normal, but I made an appointment to see a doctor in the hope I could consult with him for the next two months until I gave birth. The doctor insisted on running several tests and on receiving the results he informed me he was genuinely concerned for both my baby and me. He referred me to a specialist and advised me to go home. The girls and I flew back to New South Wales to be with my parents. At my appointment with the specialist, he also expressed concern for our wellbeing. My little one was in breach position, which can be risky for both baby and mother at the time of birth.

In the midst of all of this concern, I heard a news bulletin, stating that birth mothers who had either given up their babies voluntarily for adoption, or had had them taken by force, could have access to their birth certificates on a given date. My two older daughters and I had never ceased searching for my baby boy. Contact phone numbers were advertised so that birth mothers could phone counsellors who were especially trained and sensitive to this issue, so as to protect the privacy of all parties concerned. I contacted one such counsellor and followed her advice to the letter. After suffering the great loss of my son being taken from me and the love I still felt for him, I did not wish to hurt him in any way, nor do anything to hinder me finding even a scrap of information about him. My main concern was that he was safe, happy, and well. And of course, I yearned to meet him.

The day finally arrived and I drove to the Courthouse two hours before it was due to open and waited patiently in my car so as to obtain this precious information I had desired for so long. My heart was beating so hard I thought it would jump from my chest, as I finally descended the stairs with my son's birth certificate. With hands shaking as though they had a mind of their own, I attempted to steady myself and take in what I was reading on the paper before me. I searched frantically for a phone box and called the counsellor in order to pass on this vital information. This was the one and only link I had to my son in eighteen years. Finally, I had found him. He had been raised in the country, not far from where he was born. The counsellor told me she would phone the family immediately. I drove back to my parents' house with very mixed emotions swirling though my mind. What if he had passed away? What if his parents would not give any information to the counsellor? What if he did not know he was adopted?

I knew by the tone of her voice when the counsellor finally contacted me later that day, that the news she was about to tell me, was not good. My son's adoptive parents told her that they had never revealed to him that he was adopted. They asked if I would agree to leave things as they were, as they felt that to break the news of his adoption to him at this stage in his life, would be devastating. Of course, I agreed, but with a very heavy heart. I loved him so much and only wanted what was best for him. I did not wish to hurt him or his mum and dad. I was willing to sit in the background for now. I used to be very twisted and broken over losing him, but for the past six years, I had looked at this whole situation in a new and more positive way. Especially since I'd been given the opportunity to forgive the midwife who had been with me, during labour.

I received a letter from my son's adoptive father approximately three weeks later. He told me that he and his wife had seen the advertisements I had posted in the Pix magazine for many years after my son's birth, as I searched so desperately to find him. Along with the letter were three photos. One of my son as an extremely cute two-year-old, another at eight years of age and two more recent photos. The letter ended: 'Hoping these are some consolation'. Those three photos were more precious to me than if someone had just handed me a cheque for a million dollars. I placed them in frames and displayed them in my home, proudly showing my beautiful son to everyone who visited. I had never been ashamed of telling people about him, even though others had tried to place shame upon me during my pregnancy and after his birth.

At the same time as all of this was unfolding, my poor mum was trying to deal with my father who was now in the latter stages of Alzheimer's disease. They were waiting for a place to become available in a nursing home in the area, and due to my mum now suffering with secondary breast cancer in her bones, the doctor was doing everything in his power to hasten the process, so as to help ease the burden for her.

Things did not improve in the latter part of my pregnancy, so the specialist advised that my husband should return from Western Australia. He came home just in time, and on the 2nd May, 1988, I gave birth to another beautiful baby girl. Although there were complications during labour, we both recovered well.

Our newest addition was only three weeks old when sickness came upon my second youngest, very suddenly. One night she began to fit and fell to the floor, convulsing uncontrollably. As my husband and I knelt beside her, helpless to do anything except move whatever could harm her out of the way, my mother called the ambulance. It seemed to take forever before we heard the haunting sounds of sirens cutting through the darkness as they came towards my parent's house. My little five-year-old girl was still fitting when they arrived. They placed her in the back of the ambulance with a paramedic, while I rode in the front with my new baby, as we sped to the hospital. On arrival, my little girl was raced through a set of swinging doors, while I paced anxiously up and down outside the room, holding my baby.

A short time later, a doctor approached and told me that they had the seizure under control. When we went to see her, she was fast asleep. I was devastated. Why did this happen? The following day when I went back to the hospital, staff told me that she had experienced several more grand mal seizures and that they were running tests. I was asked if I could possibly be with her twenty-four hours a day in the hospital, until they could find out why the seizures were occurring so frequently. Sometimes she had up to a dozen or more within a twenty-four-hour period. They moved a fold-up bed into the ward beside her little bed and provided a crib for my baby. This is where we stayed for the next two or three weeks. Finally, the doctors found a medication that seemed to lessen the regularity of the seizures, and we were allowed to return home. I was informed that she had temporal lobe epilepsy and that she would most likely be medicated for life. For the next six months or so, the seizures still occurred infrequently, often coinciding with stressful situations within our family. When our baby was three months old, my husband and I decided to relocate to Brisbane, Queensland, as he had been unsuccessful in securing a job since returning from Western Australia.

## Chapter Sixteen

## Obsession, Dysfunction and Heartache

### —1988 to 1998—

We rented a home in a beachside suburb in Brisbane with our two little ones, and my second eldest daughter. John secured a job with a construction company offering 'shut down' work only. This meant that between jobs, he was unemployed for up to six weeks at a time, which was a struggle for us financially. As much as I hate to admit this, I began to steal from him once again, in order to provide meals for our family each day.

A couple of months after we moved, I became so desperate to stop the craziness going on in my head, that I almost went into frenzy mode, attending different churches and meeting again with members of the Hare Krishna movement. I was still in pursuit of God and whatever else I thought could possibly bring some joy to my life. But I began to feel as though I was fragmenting myself by searching here and seeking there in different places. No matter how hard I tried, I could never find the answer, the Truth I so desperately sought.

One day a male relative through marriage came to pay us a visit and we invited him to stay the night. John and the man I will call Eric, were having a few drinks together, so after dinner, I made up a bed on the lounge for our visitor and retired early in order to catch up on some sleep. Our baby was only a few months old at the time and her normal routine was to wake at least three times before morning for a feed. Our five-year-old climbed into her bed, gave her baby sister a hug and kiss and settled down for the night. She normally shared with her older sister, but was sleeping in the room alone that night, as her sister had gone away for the weekend. I retired to the main bedroom, placed my baby in her crib and went to sleep.

During the night I was aware of my husband coming to bed and the baby waking. Once I changed and fed her, I settled her in beside me and went back to sleep. Just before dawn, I woke to find my very distressed five-year-old trying to climb into bed next to her little sister. I sensed something was not right, and so as not to wake John, I took my baby and little girl to the kitchen, where she dissolved into tears and for a short while was inconsolable.

I just hugged and hugged her and when she settled down a little, I asked her what the matter was. She told me in between outbursts of distraught weeping, that she was not allowed to tell anyone what had happened to her through the night. I do not wish to go into lengthy detail, except to say that eventually she revealed how Eric had 'hurt' her in her bed, then told her that she was not allowed to tell, or else he would harm her. When she explained what he had done, I knew the man we had trusted and invited to stay over on our lounge, had sexually assaulted our little girl. I ran frantically to her bedroom and found Eric's wallet lying open on the floor beside her bed.

I instantly felt sick as memories of the sexual abuse I had suffered as a child, flashed through my mind. My daughter was suffering, and it was all so unfair. It was no longer the old days when you kept sexual abuse a secret. Through no fault of her own, my little girl had been assaulted by nothing less than a monster. I woke my husband and told him what had happened, and amongst his protests and threats to leave me if I called the police, I rang them anyway. In his desperation to attempt to make me change my story before they arrived, he phoned both his mum and mine, telling them what had taken place and that I had called the authorities.

Both my mother-in-law and my mother spoke to me on the phone and told me they were horrified that I would involve the law. Both stated that by doing so, I would bring shame on the family. They may as well have been talking to a brick wall. My mission was to try to find some sort of justice for my little girl. Justice I never received, due to the times I had lived in. I wondered how many others were abused by the very same people who had assaulted me, because no one spoke up and told the truth.

The police arrived and took my little daughter and me to the local hospital, where very unpleasant tests were undertaken to determine the extent of her injuries and to obtain the necessary evidence to substantiate that this event had actually taken place. On examination, the physical evidence of the sexual abuse Eric had inflicted on her, was horrific. Swabs were taken and bed linen sent to be tested and analysed in order to gain further evidence.

After we left the hospital, the police drove us straight to the station, in order for my daughter and me to give our statements. It was heart wrenching to sit and listen as this beautiful, innocent little child explained to police what had happened to her the previous night. This was so wrong. My young daughter had been the victim of a predator, just so that he could satisfy his own sick desires. It took twelve months for this case to be heard in the Supreme court in Brisbane, Queensland.

Because I was a witness, I was prevented from being present when my then six-year-old was questioned by a defence barrister, in front of a full jury, about the events that had taken place in her bedroom, on the night she was sexually assaulted. My eldest daughter was allowed in the court room, and it broke her heart to see her little sister treated as though she was an adult. She was totally discredited by the defence barrister as she spoke of the events that had unfolded on that terrible night, twelve months previously. He used his adult and professional status to intimidate her, accusing her of making up this whole story, due to the fact she could not remember the exact date that all this had taken place. Eventually he bullied and intimidated her so much with his non-stop barrage of questions, that she ended up agreeing with him that she had made this whole thing up. She just could not bear to stand in his presence any longer.

But there was more than enough forensic evidence for a conviction. All the test results were, without a shadow of a doubt, conclusive. Yet, this predator was only sentenced to eighteen months jail, with seven months non-parole, because the judge determined that, the 'poor man' was drunk and therefore did not know what he was doing. I felt the leniency of the judge towards this man was so unfair in light of what he had put my little girl through. Not to mention the potential to impact in a negative way any future relationship she might have with a male partner.

I could have remained silent and just brushed this all under the carpet and forgotten about it. But I knew that the scars of sexual abuse run deep. Despite all the evidence convicting Eric of his heinous crime, *some* people stood by him. Some who I thought of as friends; people who actually attended court and heard the evidence over a three-day period, turned on me as though I had caused this man to go to prison for no reason. My only allies who were physically present with me at this time were my sister, older daughters, my true friends and the detectives from Juvenile Aid who drove us to and from court each day.

Then, just as I was beginning to feel a little relieved that it was all over, I began receiving threatening phone calls and an abusive letter from the perpetrator's family. Unfortunately, my husband did not support me either. I could see no other choice at the time, so I took the children and walked away from my marriage for good. It was now 1990, and we moved to be closer to my two older daughters. Not long after we had settled in, my eldest daughter gave birth to my first grandchild, a baby girl. She then went on to have another little girl in 1997, followed by my first grandson in 1998.

My older daughters and granddaughter lived two streets from where I resided with my two little girls. My youngest daughter and granddaughter were just two years apart in age and as they grew up, they became great mates. My second youngest daughter had settled into school, so I decided I would like to get super fit and lose some weight. There was a gym nearby with a child-minding service for my little one and before long I was participating in up to three different classes per day. I was obsessed with trying to change my outward appearance. It wasn't as though I was carrying any extra weight to begin with, but after a while, my muscles became more defined. Because that made me feel a lot better about my appearance than I had in years, I strived even more, spending all of my free time at the gym.

I became friends with a neighbour who had two children the same age as my younger girls. Our kids played together, either at her house or mine, after school and on weekends. But I began to dread their visits, even though they were lovely children and very well behaved. Each time they came, it seemed they were not satisfied with just selecting toys from my daughters' three toy boxes. Instead, they emptied the entire contents of each one onto my lounge room floor and mixed all the toys together as they played with them.

Now, to the average person, that probably would not be such a big deal. But it made me feel physically sick to see such a mess. When it was time to pack the toys away, the next-door kids were very willing to help, and in no time the floor was clear of the mess once again. Immediately after they returned home, I emptied the toy boxes completely and sorted through the toys, placing soft ones in their own box, figurines and other small toys together, and miscellaneous others that were the same size, in their own box. I was obsessed about this and passed my obsession on to my little ones. They made sure when it was just the two of them playing together, that they only selected from each toy box what they wished to play with at the time, and they put the toys back into the 'correct' box when they had finished with them.

This was not my only obsession. When I felt stressed, I cleaned my already clean house from top to bottom. Nothing remained that was not dusted, vacuumed, and mopped. Everything in my housing commission house, received a spring clean at least two to three times per week and on the other days, I cleaned normally. If I was not cleaning, I was at the gym. I did not realise just how obsessed I was becoming with everything I did. It began to feel as though I was driven and that if I did not keep going, something terrible may happen to me. I decided to seek help and have some counselling to try to sort my head out, so to speak. After a couple of sessions, I felt great as I started to put into place the strategies the counsellor suggested, to help me to deal with my life.

That was, until while I was in the middle of answering a question he asked me, I happened to glance at my feet and noticed, to my horror, that one of them was not placed correctly within the carpet square. I had somehow moved my foot and it was now half in one square and half in another. So, I moved it back into the square. It had always been important to me that my feet were never to be across a line. I could remember being like this when I first attended school as a four-and-a-half-year-old.

My friends and I used to sing a little jingle back then, 'Don't step on a crack, or you'll break your mother's back'.

My counsellor enquired as to why I had moved my foot. I was very embarrassed as I explained to him that my feet must always be within a square. His next question shocked me. He asked if I had ever been sexually abused. I vehemently denied the fact. With that, he told me he could no longer help me, unless I was willing to tell him the truth. He explained that he did not need to know any details of the abuse, but he could not help me, unless I was totally honest with him about whether it had happened or not. I broke down and admitted the truth.

From that day on, my very patient counsellor worked with me at least once a week and kindly told me that I was 'neurotic' as well as displaying lots of other 'dysfunctional, atypical and abnormal behavioural traits'. At the time he reassured me, telling me not to be ashamed of my diagnosis but to embrace it as he could help me if I would work with him. I was so grateful that I had finally found someone I trusted enough to confide in. Gradually with his help, I began to feel as though I could conquer the world. Then I met a man who was quite different from my other partners. He had a stable job, was lovely to my children and treated me like a princess. I found this very disconcerting, but my counsellor assured me that this was the way a potential partner should treat me. After a few months of dating, my new boyfriend asked if I would consider living with him.

I was unsure of what I should do. It seemed to me my new male friend was not overly exciting. In fact, sometimes I thought that his lovely manner and the way he treated my children and me was downright boring. But, with my counsellor's assurance that the man's behaviour towards me sounded very normal, I decided to take a chance, and my youngest girls and I moved into his home. which was approximately three hours from our previous address. My older daughters visited from time to time, the eldest finding employment in the same town and settling there along with my granddaughter. Eventually she met a man, and they married. Unfortunately, I broke up with my partner after nine months and moved into a rental home with my two younger children. My ex-partner was too nice to me and I did not understand how and why he was like this. I thought at the time it was all just an act and that he would change suddenly and begin to treat me badly.

While my two youngest daughters were at pre-school and school, I began studying naturopathy via correspondence. Both my parents had sadly passed away by this time and had left an inheritance for my siblings and me. My desire had been to study and work in the field of natural therapies, ever since my second eldest daughter's ill health had dramatically improved, when, out of sheer desperation, I had consulted a naturopath seventeen years previously. Now I could finally afford to study the Diploma level course through a college on the Sunshine Coast, Queensland. It was a requirement of the Diploma that I complete some of the modules face to face. I really enjoyed the content of the course, especially the Remedial Massage component. A good friend of mine and her daughter accompanied my girls and me to the coast whenever I needed to attend practical lectures and my friend kindly looked after my girls while I was in class.

One day, whilst I was participating in one of the practical massage classes, the college principal approached me and asked if I would be interested in becoming an assistant massage teacher. I loved the Sunshine Coast, and this seemed like an opportunity too good to miss. I decided to accept her offer and move there to be closer to the college and work. Whilst being excited to be beginning a new adventure, I was also sad to be moving away from my older girls and my grandchildren. The friends I had made since moving to this small mining town decided to give me a going away party at a local hotel. It was held the week prior to my leaving. On the night of the party, I went to buy myself a drink at the bar and met a man. After chatting for a while, he invited me to have dinner with him the next evening and after dating a couple more times before I left, he asked me to be his girlfriend. I moved to the Sunshine Coast with my two youngest daughters and my new partner began to visit from time to time. Even though I was unsure about whether or not I loved him, when he asked me to marry him six months later, I accepted, and we became engaged.

I enjoyed my new role as an assistant massage teacher and decided to discontinue my studies in Naturopathy. By now I had completed my Diploma of Remedial Massage and was working in my own clinic. At the same time, I was studying other styles of massage as well, with the idea of becoming as qualified as I could possibly be, in this field.

Whilst living on the coast, I discovered a Buddhist temple and decided to pursue my search for Truth by attending lectures and meditation each Wednesday. Sometimes my youngest daughter accompanied me and we sat upon cushions on the floor, listening intently to the Tibetan lama. He went into great detail as he explained how to live a peaceful life. Although I must have gone to that temple for the best part of a year, I never seemed to be able to come into that state of being. It seemed I was living in fight or flight mode most days, and added to the anxiety, I was experiencing uncertainty about my decision to commit to my latest partner. His visits became less frequent which caused me to feel rejected and lonely.

I began to have a glass of wine with dinner each night. I discovered alcohol helped me to relax a little and as time went on, I increased my intake in order for it to have the same effect. Occasionally, friends offered me marijuana, which totally wiped me out if I smoked it at the same time I was drinking. While in an altered mind state, whether it be from alcohol, drugs or meditation, I could escape the guilt and shame from my past for a short time. But reality does not just magically go away. I still had to face the emotional turmoil once the euphoric state of consciousness wore off. Unfortunately, around this time, I began witnessing my older children making decisions which caused them grief. After ending a very abusive relationship, my second eldest daughter's ex-partner attempted to kill her. He tampered with the brakes of her new car, causing them to fail as she drove one day. He then tried to run her over on a pedestrian crossing and set fire to a friend's house where she had sought shelter. Thanks be to God in his last attempt to end her life, he was foiled through a covert operation carried out by undercover detectives.

I had never felt that I deserved to be treated with love and respect within a relationship and so by my example, I was unwittingly teaching my children to accept the unacceptable. The realisation of this was so obvious, yet I did not see it at the time. I just kept accepting disrespect and ill treatment, bending over backwards to be however or whoever my partner at the time expected me to be. All the while feeling helpless and hopeless, not knowing how to change my situation. But deep down I knew if I could find God, one way or another, He would help me.

It was around this time my eldest daughter kindly offered us accommodation at her rental home, located on a ten-acre property six hours north of where we now resided. The College I was working for had since gone bankrupt, and even though I had built up my own successful massage business, I missed my older children and grandchildren. They all resided in and around the area I would be moving to, so I accepted my daughter's offer and my younger girls and I relocated once again.

# Chapter Seventeen

## Roller Coaster Ride

### —1998-2001—

The property was nestled amongst rugged mountains with a picturesque rainforest-edged creek. The area was known for its locally hand-crafted pottery, a unique resort, and numerous other attractions. My youngest daughter attended the small primary school and we soon settled in and were invited to many functions. I began massaging some of the local people, swapping treatments for homegrown fruit and vegetables. After a few months, I decided to teach again, so I rented a room at a health clinic in the closest town and began instructing a class. Once my students completed thirty hours of Swedish massage, they had the option to put to use the skills they had learnt on family and friends or continue in order to obtain a certificate. This would then qualify them to open their own clinic.

After we relocated, my fiancé rarely visited, always seeming to have an excuse as to the reason why. One year I saw him on three separate occasions, a total of thirty-one days in all. He told me he was busy with his work and I believed him at first. Due to the nature of his job, he was often required to work in remote areas throughout Australia. Many times, I suggested that I home-school my youngest daughter in order to travel with him. But he made it noticeably clear that this was not an option. My friends spoke to me about the situation, expressing their concern that maybe he was living a double life. I started to believe that what they were saying was possibly true. They also made reference to the amount of time my fiancé and I spent apart, which caused me to think about whether this relationship was even worth pursuing.

The tumultuous state of my mind often caused me to wake in the early hours of the morning. The very idea of my fiancé possibly cheating on me was a real concern and I began making up stories in my head about how he may be doing this. Who else, besides me, was he sharing his life with? When the voices in my head and the pain of rejection and deep hurt overwhelmed me, I worked obsessively to escape and distract myself. Everything I put my hand to had to be done perfectly. The lecture notes I prepared for my massage students are a good example of this. I wrote the lecture, delivered it to the class, then rewrote it again. This was not only for my own satisfaction in knowing I had presented a perfect lecture, but also so my students could have the opportunity to be perfect therapists, by the time they had finished the course. In my mind, nothing I ever did was good enough. I was slowly driving myself crazy. I started praying to the God of my childhood and told Him all my troubles. I asked for His help and just left it at that. But as my emotional state spiralled even more out of control, I felt the need to reach out to a friend and she invited me to attend her Church. This gave me some peace, however, if only for a short time. I also formed friendships with some of the local ladies in our area and experienced glimpses of fun and adventure amidst the craziness of my mind. We swam in creeks and under waterfalls, rode our bicycles through the state forest and sometimes had meals together.

In order for my students to put into practice the remedial massage techniques I taught them, I would invite some of my clients and friends with diverse physical ailments, to my place, for them to practise their massage skills. We all enjoyed these days immensely. Amongst the seriousness, as the students diligently worked on releasing areas of muscle tension and tightness, there were often outbursts of laughter. For example, if someone a student was massaging began to snore loudly, or the session when a student named a muscle in the neck, as one that was actually in the buttock area. During our lunch break, we sat on the veranda together, chatting and laughing about all manner of topics. I looked forward to these days as they helped me to forget my troubles for a few hours at least.

One night in September, 2000, I was almost asleep when I felt prompted to check my breasts for lumps. I had been teaching my class that day about the old-fashioned way of healing, using poultices made of herbs, to treat various illnesses. I shared a recipe with them for removing breast tumours and another remedy to apply to the breast after the tumour came out to heal the area. I was shocked when I felt a very distinct pea–size lump in my right breast. I found it hard to believe that what I was actually feeling may be a reason for concern. After all, I lived an extremely healthy lifestyle to the degree of being obsessive regarding my family's diet and how much I exercised. I woke up the next morning and walked to the small, palm-lined creek on the property with my two dogs and cat following closely behind me. I entered the water, sat on the sandy bottom of the creek and prayed a profoundly serious prayer to God, asking Him to please heal me. After I finished praying, I suddenly remembered a question the pastor of the church I had begun attending, had asked me a few weeks previously.

He said, 'If you were to die tonight, do you know where you would go'?

I did not have an answer. I hoped I would go to heaven. But I had not given it too much thought until now.

After I left the creek, I dried myself off and was walking back up the bank, when I heard a soft small voice speak to me. The voice said something like this: 'You have cancer and need surgery'.

That was it. No more conversation. I knew I had just heard from God. I believed from what He said to me, that as much as I wanted to apply a poultice on the breast lump and remove it myself, I was to do His Will and seek medical help. So, what next? I had an obligation to see my massage students finish their qualification. I could not let them down. I chose to finish teaching the course and to not disclose to anyone, about the lump I had discovered.

One of my students was struggling to pay her tuition fees, so I asked if she would like to massage me, in lieu of what she owed. She agreed and began treating me fortnightly. During one of the massages, it was as though a dam wall suddenly let go within me. I broke down and confided in her about the lump I had found. I had no medical diagnosis at this time, but I knew I had cancer because God had told me. I decided to fast-track my students without disclosing the real reason why. I simply said I wanted them to complete their Certificate by early December so they could begin the New Year working for themselves. They agreed that this was a great idea. Tears welled in my eyes as I watched them complete their final assessment. I was so proud of them as they applied everything I had taught them over the past twelve months. On their special graduation day, I felt both sad and relieved. I certainly was going to miss our times together, but now I could finally focus on what was about to take place in my life.

I rarely visited the doctor unless my children or I were extremely sick, and a poultice or natural therapy had not fixed the condition at the time. I randomly chose a doctor from the phone book, and to my surprise, there was an appointment available the following day. Immediately the examination was completed, the doctor ordered a breast screen to be done as soon as possible. After the screen, I was recalled to have a fine needle biopsy. Then followed an appointment to see a surgeon. The surgeon explained he would remove a seven-centimetre section from my breast, just as a precaution. Even though there were abnormal cells in the biopsy result, he did not think I had cancer. I knew differently. On the day of surgery, my second eldest daughter accompanied me to the hospital. While I was in recovery, the surgeon came and told me that pathology on the section he had taken from my breast, contained cancer cells to its borders. He explained that I would need to have a lumpectomy followed by radiotherapy. I was not at all surprised. Following a series of blood tests and further examination, my surgeon asked permission to perform another biopsy at the base of my breast. The result was also positive. Lumpectomy and radiotherapy were no longer options, so I was booked into the hospital for a total mastectomy.

These arrangements were made one week out from Christmas and to my surprise, my partner returned home to support me. On the day of scheduled surgery, I rose early and walked to the creek. It was such a beautiful environment. A place I had come to many times lately to sit alone and cry, as I did not want my youngest daughter to witness the fear I was experiencing due to the uncertainty of our future. Suddenly, I felt a need to be baptised. I submerged my entire body beneath the cool water for a second or two, then prayed and told God that it was my belief that I had just baptised myself. And no matter what happened, I was counting on Him to look after me.

I asked Him, 'Please God, don't take me yet. I still have my youngest daughter to raise'.

I told Him if He decided my time on earth was over, could He make sure that she was taken care of and that I went to heaven and not to that other awful place called hell I was told about when I was a child. I apologised to Him for not looking after myself and for not being the person He had created me to be. I had always been a 'yes' person, for fear of displeasing others. Now I believed I was suffering the consequences of not standing up for myself and instead holding onto unspoken words of resentment.

When I arrived home five days after surgery, my partner told me he had to return to work. After he left, my daughters, one of my sisters and a girlfriend stayed with me until I was well enough to look after myself. I am not one to sit about; I purposefully did all the exercises the doctor and physiotherapist prescribed for me, plus some of my own. Even though I had been obsessive before the operation with sourcing organic foods where possible and eating a healthy diet, I became even more so. When I returned to the surgeon to have my stitches taken out, he informed me that he was 95% certain that he had removed all the cancer. He suggested chemotherapy as an option, to mop up any cells that may remain. I decided against this due to the dreadful effect it had had on my beautiful mother. I believed God had given me a reprieve and I was so grateful to Him for healing me.

Approximately five weeks after the operation, I received a phone call from a person I barely knew, who told me my fiancé was leading a double life. When I confronted my partner about this, he vehemently denied the accusations. I was devastated and immediately broke off our engagement. Each day I listened to him as he pleaded with me that he was telling the truth, and that he had done nothing wrong. Eventually, after a few weeks, I foolishly allowed him back into my life and the lives of my precious children and grandchildren. I was so naïve, believing everything he told me. Sadly, my eldest daughter and her husband who owned the property where we lived, separated. I found a rental home in a small village not far away, and wonderful friends of mine helped my youngest daughter and me to relocate. My second youngest, who was pregnant with her first baby, moved in with us.

## Chapter Eighteen

## Running from God

### —2001-2007—

My doctor was amazed at how quickly I recovered from the mastectomy. I was well enough to resume massaging within weeks of leaving hospital. The reality of how fearful I had been when I first received the cancer diagnosis and how fervently I prayed to God to save my life, seemed to have completely slipped my mind. I had even bargained with Him at the time, that if He answered my prayer, I would reduce my workload, stop being a 'yes' person and try to look after myself. I believed without a doubt that God had prompted me to have surgery and that He was the reason I had received such an incredible prognosis after the operation. I thanked Him for His goodness and mercy for saving me, then proceeded to slip back into the very same self-destructive way of living that I was accustomed to, hardly giving Him a second thought. But God had not forgotten about me. He had my attention when I thought I was going to die, and He was not about to give up on me now. He had always been at work in my life, even though for the most part, I was totally unaware of Him.

As far as I was concerned, I was now healed and ready to move on using a slightly different approach. I had been involved in the occult for as long as I could remember and now the New Age movement was 'alive and well' and truly in full swing. I attempted to find true happiness by focusing on me. I tried to think positive thoughts and pamper and nurture myself. I soon realised that this requires quite a healthy bank account, so I began to meditate again, hoping to bring peace and calm into my life. But God had other plans and He often uses people to bring our attention to Himself.

Through my work I met a lady and her husband who were both pastors. I will call them Mary and Jack. Mary became a regular client and it was not long before she began inviting me to listen to visiting evangelists or guest speakers at their church. I sometimes accepted her invitation. The very first time I called in out of curiosity, I could not help but compare it to the church I had attended as a child. Our church had been very conservative, but this was a full-on Pentecostal church, and I thought they had all lost their minds. Most of the congregation appeared to be extremely excited, for some reason or another, about God. Some even clapped their hands and jumped up and down. Several times during the service, people ran through the Church waving flags. They randomly sang out to encourage the pastor or speaker with loud shouts of 'Amen', 'preach it brother' or, 'Hallelujah'. After my initial experience, I tried hard to resist Mary's invitations. But she had a way with words, and I was a people pleaser searching for 'something', just anything to make me feel better.

Sometimes when Mary came for a massage, I became upset and a little angry with her. She talked about Jesus too much for my liking, and to be honest, I was so resistant to this kind of talk that I wanted to block my ears and run from her presence. But there was another side of her that both puzzled yet attracted me. We began meeting for coffee occasionally and quite often as we sat and chatted, she would answer her phone to someone obviously in need. She would then apologise, briefly explaining the urgency of the situation she needed to attend to, and leave. I thought it was a bit rude of her at first. But as it happened on a number of occasions, I could not help but notice that she always put everyone else's needs before her own.

As much as I hated to admit it, Mary was starting to grow on me. I observed her closely, trying to work out what it was that made her so different. I thought *I* was a generous and kind person, but she was even more so. It seemed that her husband Jack and she had certainly been through their own share of heartache and pain, but even with their many trials, they appeared to cope well. They were noticeably confident and sure of themselves, but at the same time, they were humble. It was as though they identified with something or someone that I did not quite understand at this time. I was beginning to question *my* identity. Did I even have one? Who was I? What was life all about? Our relationship continued, and though this lady mostly drove me crazy, I was now seeing her in a vastly different light.

I loved spending time with family, and mine seemed to be growing at a rapid rate. As well as my eldest daughter's three children, there were now a few new additions. A baby grandson and granddaughter born in 2002, a grandson in 2004, followed by another granddaughter in 2006. And I must not forget to mention Snooki, Frankie, Gus and Trevor, my fur grandchildren.

My friends were still expressing their concern about the relationship between my fiancé and me. The trust I had once had in him was all but gone, so I began to look for a way out. The past twelve years since we had been together had been filled with mental anguish that had gradually increased like a tsunami building deep in the ocean far from land, that had to crash and destroy somewhere, someday. I had foolishly depended on him to make me happy no matter the cost. Except now our dysfunctional relationship was beginning to cost me my very soul. I ended it once and for all. As I look back at my journal and reflect on what was happening in my life at this time, I find it hard to believe what I am reading. I barely recognise myself as being the person who wrote such things. I question the reason why I allowed myself to be treated so badly up until now. My handwriting is so small in my journal that I can barely read it, which reminds me of how low my self-esteem was back then. The very ink on the pages seemed to drip with guilt, sadness, and shame.

After the breakup, I initially felt very lonely, until a few months later when a girlfriend introduced me to Internet dating. I was excited at first by the prospect of possibly meeting a loving partner – someone who could make me feel good about myself. Soon, I was dating again, although it was not long before I realised that no one could give me whatever it was I was so desperately pursuing. In desperation, I tried reading the Bible, but it made no sense to me. Lately, church was somewhere I sometimes went if it was raining or overcast and I could not spend time at the beach. I exercised excessively, worked excessively and ended up feeling like nothing came even close to filling the emptiness inside me. Sometimes I went out to dinner with friends, but once we had eaten and they returned home, I stayed out by myself. I often sat in bars alone, drinking alcohol until I felt the edge easing from the emotional pain and loneliness I was feeling at the time.

I felt very blessed to have such wonderful, caring daughters, their partners and my grandchildren who loved and accepted me, no matter the mess I was in. But even though I knew my family was there for me, I still hungered for that someone or something that seemed impossible for me to find. Who was I? And to whom did I belong? Others told me who they thought I was, and I was growing weary of trying to be whoever anyone wanted me to be at the time. I began attending the local Uniting Church with a couple of my grandchildren but decided not to commit to something I did not fully understand. I was running from God and I knew it.

## Chapter Nineteen

## *Another Miraculous Healing*

### —2007-2010—

As time passed, Mary became even more persistent with her untamed desire to see me more regularly in church. I wanted to get cross with her but just could not bring myself to do so. She continually spoke of Jesus and His Mercy, Love and Grace for people. There was something about her that was drawing me to want to be in her presence more often. I began noticing that other Christians I was acquainted with were somehow different as well. Most had an unshakable confidence that I could not fathom. Not a lot seemed to worry them. Especially once they said; 'I'll go and pray about this'. Or, 'Let me ask The Lord about that and I will get back to you'. It seemed to me that they checked in with God about everything they ever did. Instead of wishing to be as far away from Christians as I possibly could be, I found myself wanting to hang out with them.

Around this time, another dear Christian friend and her husband suffered a great and totally unexpected loss. Their baby passed away within days of his birth. I attended the funeral and was amazed at how they coped amidst the sadness and grief they were obviously experiencing. They appeared to handle this whole situation in an almost surreal way. I was in awe of them and wanted whatever they seemed to have in my life. It was as though they still had 'hope' somehow and all was not lost. Despite the fact that they were grieving, it was like they were receiving some kind of strength and comfort from a supernatural source. I yearned for this to somehow rub off on to me and sought to be in their presence whenever and wherever possible.

I began to seek a deeper understanding of who God really is, but once it became evident to me that I could have an intimate relationship with Him, I became fearful and pulled back. This is extremely hard to explain, but it was as though once I began to experience His great love, I was overwhelmed, felt unworthy and could not accept it. How could God pour out this incredible love, such as I had never experienced before, on a sinner such as me? To be honest, it frightened me so much that I turned away and slowly drifted back into my old lifestyle once again. I still attended church now and then and carried on with my obsessions and perfectionism. I distracted myself in any way I could and fled from the beautiful Spiritual love that God so wanted to lavish on me.

Over the next six years, I began taking a few inexpensive overseas holidays. It was refreshing to visit new places, explore other cultures and relax a little. After returning from one of these trips, I decided to have a mammogram and ultra-sound. My decision to do this surprised me as I had no obvious symptoms and was not a fan of undergoing tests at the best of times. I obtained the necessary referral from my doctor and went ahead anyway. The next day I received a phone call advising me to come back to the clinic for further investigation. A lesion had shown up on both mammogram and ultra-sound. A fine needle biopsy was performed, and the results were positive for cancer. My doctor arranged for me to have surgery the very next week. My life was beginning to feel like a commonly occurring nightmare with longer periods of drama and fewer times without. I was filled with fear and fell to my knees once again, pleading with God to please take this cancer from me.

I noticed an advertisement in the local paper about an evangelist who was visiting our town to preach and perform 'healing ministries', at three different locations. On Saturday morning prior to my scheduled surgery, I decided to attend one of the advertised venues at an undercover lunch area at a school close to where I lived. When I arrived, I could not help but notice that the atmosphere was charged with an excited expectation, almost as though something wonderful was about to take place. I immediately had a change of heart and wanted nothing more than to return to the safety of my own home. I was already anxious and upset due to the diagnosis I had received only days earlier, and the hype and excitement at this meeting was making me feel very uneasy. I became almost paranoid, concerned that someone may ask me why I had attended. Would people assume that I was sick? It surprised me to see so many gathered together to hear the message the evangelist was about to bring. Suddenly, a lady I had met in church noticed me. She beckoned excitedly and gestured for me to come and sit with her. Now I really felt trapped. I had no sooner taken my seat when a man appeared from amidst the crowd, leapt onto the stage, introduced himself as the visiting evangelist and began to talk about Jesus, saying, 'Jesus can heal the sick. He is alive and is here in our midst today'.

Now I really felt the urge to leave immediately. I had no desire to sit and listen to this microphone-wielding so-called evangelist. But the place was packed and I couldn't see a way out. He spoke about how some people who had attended the meeting the previous night had received prayer and were healed. He asked if any of them were present and several walked forward and gave testimonies about how Jesus had healed them from all kinds of ailments. One lady claimed that she had been wheelchair-bound for many years and after receiving prayer, Jesus healed her, and she could now walk normally. I had to admit that I had observed this lady in her wheelchair, many times in our village. I thought at the time that these so-called miraculous healings must have been purely coincidental.

After the evangelist presented the Gospel and healing ministry of Jesus, he invited anyone who was sick or incapacitated in any way to come forward. People moved along the rows and out into the aisle like flies. I couldn't believe it. I tried to use this moment as an opportunity to escape. I said goodbye to my friend and stood in line in the aisle behind a very tall man with a sick child draped over his shoulder. My plan was that as the crowd moved forward, I would exit down one of the half empty rows I could see ahead and make a quick dash to my car. This wasn't to be. The evangelist, along with his microphone, was in my face as I was hatching my getaway plan.

He pushed past at least ten people saying all the while: 'Jesus wants to heal a certain person here. And it is you,' he said, as he stood before me. He then spoke into his microphone and said, 'So, what sickness is in your body that you would like Jesus to heal today'?

Why was he making a spectacle of me by singling me out from the crowd? With that, he placed the microphone in front of my face, waiting for me to answer. I did not wish to speak about my 'sickness', in front of one hundred plus people and whispered my concern about this to him. He respected this and asked me quietly what he could pray about for me. I told him that I was having surgery in four days to have cancer removed from my breast for the second time. With that he handed his intrusive microphone to someone else, placed his hands on my shoulders and prayed. I was embarrassed, even though he spoke quietly. I cannot remember anything he said, except, 'Jesus is going to heal you'. I then felt heat move through my body. The evangelist asked me to return again that night to a different venue he was speaking at, as he wanted to pray for me again.

I was out of there as quickly as my legs could carry me. What on earth had just taken place? I thought he was such a charlatan. But what was the heat I had clearly felt? I didn't return for follow-up prayer that night. I was both sceptical and a little fearful. On Monday morning, I received a phone call from the lady I had sat with at the meeting on Saturday. She told me she had attended the night meeting the evangelist had invited me to, and as I had not come, he prayed with her for a miraculous healing for me. I found this all very strange.

A few days later, I underwent surgery to remove the tumour, then waited in fear for the pathology result. The next week the surgeon called and told me he needed to see me as soon as possible, so I made an appointment for the next day. This is what I wrote in my journal on the 26/11/2007, the day prior to the appointment:

'I feel sick to the pit of my stomach. I am shaking and can't think. I am so upset. Oh, what has happened? What is happening in my life? I am strong though. But today I feel weak. Please God; help me to get through today. Amen'.

Because I assumed the news the doctor was about to give me was not going to be good and that I was about to die, I asked one of my close friends to accompany me to my appointment for support. I did not wish for my family to be traumatised any more than they already were, with what I thought would be a negative outcome. Negative it was. No cancer. The doctor was perplexed. He had two pathology reports in front of him on his desk. One from the fine needle biopsy, stating that a malignant tumour existed, and the other, the results from the removed lump, saying there was no cancer present.

God certainly had my attention. This wonderful outcome could only be due to the Evangelist praying and asking Jesus to heal me.

There was no other explanation. How could I only half believe that He existed now? I began pondering on the other times when He had obviously intervened and saved me. It all began when I was five days old and almost died. Then again when I was twelve and nearly drowned in the farm creek. All the risks I took as a teenager, accepting lifts with strangers and also with friends who drove their own vehicles, while under the influence of drugs and or/alcohol. When my children and I, through sheer necessity, hid in ditches in the dark of night. The times when we hitchhiked on dangerous highways, trying to run from domestic violence. God used others to help me when I was chased by my partner with a gun. My neighbour assisted my children and me to finally escape the situation for good. I could go on and on about the miraculous interventions that had occurred in my life, which could only have been orchestrated by God. There was too much evidence now that there was a loving and caring Father in Heaven, who was looking out for my family and me.

But the very thought of moving closer to Him still terrified me. I would have to change so much. So, I chose to attempt to block from my mind, once again, God's mighty love and compassion for me. But He was not giving up, and little by little, He was leaving His mark on me. Mary wasn't giving up, either. I thought at the time that she and God must have had some sort of agreement between them on how to introduce me and bring me into a personal relationship with Him. She was determined for me to come to her church and I kept using the excuse that there was no Sunday school for my grandchildren. Then one day she informed me that her church had set one up. I had run out of excuses.

## Chapter Twenty

# The Simple Believes Every Word

### —2010-2012—

*'The simple believes every word,
But the prudent considers well his steps'.*

**—Proverbs 14:15—**

Mary and Jack were extremely excited when I told them that after receiving prayer prior to surgery, the surgeon had informed me that there was no cancer present in the tissue he removed from my breast. I started attending their church with my grandchildren, and after a couple of Sunday meetings, I began to feel an overwhelming sense of deep regret that I had hardly ever taken my own children to church. Yet my parents had made this their priority for my siblings and me, despite the busyness of life on our dairy farm.

As a child, my understanding of God was that He was an angry and judgemental spirit in heaven who watched my every move and noted my mistakes in a black book. Of course, I no longer believed this. Ever since my son had been taken from me, I prayed that we would be re-united one day. I also prayed whenever my loved ones or I were in any kind of trouble. I began asking Mary and Jack questions about how I could have a personal relationship with God. They said that first I had to acknowledge and believe that He loved me so much that He sent His only Son Jesus, to die for me on a cross to take away my sin, then raised Him from the dead. I was to repent of my sins, ask Jesus to forgive me, then invite Him to come into my heart to be my Lord and Saviour. Up until now my relationship with God had been one-sided. I told Him all of my troubles, asking that He would somehow fix the mess I had made, but only half-heartedly believing that He would. When things were going well, I barely gave God the time of day. However, things were a little different now.

When I was fifty-eight years of age, Mary and Jack guided me in a prayer and I invited Jesus to come into my heart, to be my Lord and Saviour. They baptised me in a creek and suggested I read the Bible and attend church so that I could grow spiritually and be part of a church family. I took their advice and enjoyed making new friends. I even began to notice that my thoughts were a little more positive. I started to believe that I would meet my son one day, in God's perfect timing. I had been praying for the last forty years that this would come about, daydreaming about it, but never fully believing it would happen. That was, until now. I also noticed that I was not constantly in fight or flight mode twenty-four hours of each day and I enjoyed reading the Bible for the first time in my life. But I can honestly say that I did not notice a dramatic change in my circumstances. In some ways, things actually became worse.

In church and through the Scriptures, I was learning that God wants to set us free. I understood that by asking Jesus to be my Lord and Saviour, He had taken my sin, but I was still anxious. The apostle Paul and his co-author Timothy tell us in Philippians 4:6 (NLT), 'Don't worry about anything; instead, pray about everything. Tell God what you need and thank Him for all He has done'.

Then the scripture goes on to say that if we do this, we will experience God's peace in our lives. I was giving Him some of my worries, but more often than not I would take them straight back again. I learned that although Jesus offers us Salvation as a free gift, He did not say life would suddenly become easy. He even warned that by following Him, we were to expect to be persecuted as He was, during his time on earth. But instead of going through these hard and trying times alone, we have a loving Father who tells us that He will take our burdens upon Himself and that He will guide and strengthen us no matter how hard things seem to be. He knows how we feel, because He, as Jesus Christ on this earth, (God in the flesh,) went through even greater trials. All so He could have a relationship with us.

In the book of Mathew 5:10-12), Jesus taught His disciples, saying,

'Blessed are those who are persecuted for righteousness sake, for theirs is the kingdom of heaven. Blessed are you when they revile and persecute you, and say all kinds of evil against you falsely for My sake. Rejoice and be exceedingly glad, for great *is* your reward in heaven, for so they persecuted the prophets who were before you'.

I knew in my heart without a doubt, it was Jesus who had healed me. But unfortunately, at this point in time, I still did not surrender my life fully to Him. I was so used to making all of my own decisions, that the very thought of giving God total control scared me.

It was now 2010 and my second youngest daughter, who already had a son born in 2002 and a daughter in 2006, gave birth to her third child, a little boy. Two years later in 2012, another baby girl entered the world. I felt very blessed to have such a precious family and I loved them all dearly. But I still did not feel complete. I decided to try Internet dating again. A few relationships began but then ended as quickly as they had started. It was as though God was convicting me lovingly and gently, by letting me know this was not His will for me, and that He would choose a partner for me if it was part of His plan for my life. At first, I went against this conviction, attempting to find different ways to justify what I was doing. In desperation I began searching *Christian* dating sites, thinking that maybe God would approve. In the most beautiful and wonderful way, I could feel His very Presence like a loving parent, guiding me away from this also. So, I began to bargain with Him: 'I will go to Church and read my Bible, but I still feel the need to find my perfect partner'.

Mary and Jack explained to me that even though you surrender your life to Jesus, He still gives you free will. At this early stage of my walk with Him, I felt as though I was a small child and God was my wise Father (which He is). He was offering to show me the gift of His Will for my life, but I was only taking part of that gift and rejecting the rest. I desperately wanted to receive the *entire* gift, but I also wanted what the world was offering me.

Friends of mine told me of an opportunity to crew on a yacht they had recently sold. The new owner was sailing from our coastal town to the Whitsunday islands, over a period of four-weeks. I expressed interest and my friends assured me that they had spent quite some time sailing with this man and found him to be trust-worthy and capable of making this trip. The Whitsunday islands are located off the central coast of Queensland Australia. Seventy-four islands make up this group, and most are uninhabited.

A meeting was arranged on board with the new owner, whom I will call Robert (not his real name for privacy reasons). Robert explained that he was looking for one crew member to accompany him on his trip, just to help pull the odd rope here and there, or take the helm if he was busy attending to other tasks. He took me on a tour of his yacht, pointing out two separate cabins. The cabin at the stern, he explained, was for crew, and the one at the bow was his. I enquired as to the cost of the trip, should I decide to take up this opportunity he was offering. Robert assured me that there was no cost and all I would need to provide was my own food and drinks. Wanting to be sure I was clear on his expectations of the crew member he was seeking, I asked if he expected sexual favours in return for payment, should I decide to take up this offer. I felt a little embarrassed by his reply and almost wished I had not enquired. He appeared to be shocked that I would ask such a thing and told me that he was a man of high morals and good intentions.

After the meeting, I noticed I felt sick in my stomach and was at first unsure about whether or not to go on this trip. But after a few days had passed, I imagined myself relaxing for four whole weeks and visiting sun-kissed palm tree lined islands. I brushed this sick feeling aside and began planning for what I thought would be the opportunity of a lifetime.

At this stage in my Christian walk, it did not even cross my mind to ask God what He thought about this whole situation. I was so used to making my own choices, it did not occur to me that perhaps I should be consulting Him right now. My sense of adventure prevailed over not only my own concerns, but those of my family, friends and some of my clients. As the departure date grew closer, I sometimes experienced a nagging feeling of uneasiness, but I pushed that aside as I excitedly prepared to set off. I justified it all in my head, believing that Robert was being totally honest with me about his reasons for wanting crew. I set sail with him regardless, throwing all caution to the wind so to speak. And windy it was. Robert had not thought about his safety, let alone mine, and set off in very unfavourable conditions.

My only previous sailing experience had been helping an acquaintance race a small catamaran when I was twenty-four years old. This was vastly different to what I was encountering now on this forty-five-foot monohull. I thought that we must have needed the high winds to push the yacht along faster, even though Robert appeared to be having trouble as he tried to control the billowing sails. The more the boat rocked and rolled, the more I enjoyed the whole experience, even though Robert appeared to be incredibly stressed and the waves seemed to increase in size as the day progressed. At one point I turned to look behind and was amazed at the enormous wave baring down upon us. Then to my joy, I noticed a pod of dolphins riding down the wave towards the boat. As they reached the stern, they parted into two groups, surfing along either side of the yacht and joining as one at the bow.

I was feeling rather hungry by mid-day and suggested to Robert that I go below and make us some lunch and a cup of tea. He looked at me as though I had lost my mind. It was not until I was in the galley of the boat that I realised how rough the conditions actually were. As the boat heeled to one side, I noticed the portholes were under water and at first I was tossed from one side of the cabin to the other. I finally managed to prepare lunch by bracing myself against the table. We sailed all day until we reached a picturesque bay in which we sheltered for three days from the relentless high winds. Some of the ropes from the sails had actually snapped under the pressure of the forces of nature, which had made Robert truly angry at the time, as he attempted to wrestle against the elements. I thought I had handled the rough seas well. I did not realise the danger he had placed us both in until an acquaintance of his arrived on a yacht a few days later and told me Robert should never have ventured out in such unfavourable conditions.

It was while we were sheltering in the bay that I noticed around four o'clock each afternoon, Robert would start to drink hot beer. I asked him why he did not refrigerate it and he told me he preferred to drink it warm. The trouble was, with each drink he consumed, the more he tried to seduce me into coming into his cabin to sleep with him. I was horrified and as the days went on, he became quite rude and aggressive with his incessant invitations. One day when we went ashore on one of the islands, I found a flat, thick smooth rock, just big enough to fit into the palm of my hand. I placed it into my backpack. I was becoming worried that he may try to harm me in some way, so I formulated a plan to use the stone to calm down his advances towards me if necessary. I aimed to hit him in the centre of his forehead, hopefully just knocking him unconscious for a short while. I began to sleep on deck each night, so as to avoid him as much as possible.

Robert's anger and apparent ill feeling towards me escalated, as I continued to refuse his invitations to his cabin each night. In the second week of our trip, he started preventing me from going ashore. I often met other people whilst on land, who were sailing through the islands, and he had become jealous of my relationship with them. He began to yell at me saying that I was the most naïve person he had ever met, because I believed him at our first meeting when he told me he only had the best intentions. It soon became evident to several people we met along the way, that he was jealously guarding me as though I was his possession. Some anchored their vessels close to us, as word spread through the small community of 'yachties' about his bizarre behaviour. I was often invited by crew from other boats to join them for lunch or dinner, so as to give me some reprieve. But after a while I turned down their kind invitations, due to the jealous outrage I faced from Robert each time I returned to his yacht.

The owners of these boats and their passengers observed him using binoculars to see what I was doing when I was in their company. He even accused them of trying to steal his crew. Two men in particular were so concerned for my wellbeing, that they began plotting courses with Robert each night, so they could sail in close proximity the following day in case he tried to harm me in any way. He eventually realised the reason they were doing this and put a stop to it early one morning. The two men came alongside, in readiness to sail together as we did each day. Robert informed them that we had made other plans. As they were already in transit, I watched in fear as they sailed away, the crew looking concerned as to why he had suddenly changed plans. I was soon to find that out the reason for this.

There was little to no communication between us as we sailed alone to our next destination. Just before sunset, Robert manoeuvred the yacht slowly toward what appeared to be a deserted island. Fear gripped me as I scanned the ocean frantically, hoping to see another boat in the vicinity. But we were all alone. I checked my phone and realised I had no service and remembered at the beginning of the trip, asking him why he had not reported our journey to anyone just in case something untoward happened. He informed me that it was no one else's business as to where we were.

Once we anchored, he went below and began his usual routine of consuming warm beer. I retrieved my backpack from my cabin, along with the flat rock I had found, returned to the deck and waited, praying for God to protect me. I held the rock in readiness, as I was certain it would not be long before he decided to join me and vent his anger as he did each night because of my refusal to sleep with him. But now I felt totally alone as there was no one in the vicinity to call to if necessary.

After half an hour or so, I heard him begin to curse and swear. He was incredibly angry and started yelling loudly saying that he could have been receiving $500 per day from a 'paying passenger', instead of having me on board, travelling for free. And how dare I not let him have his way with me. As he consumed more and more alcohol, his cursing became louder and more frightening. I knew I had to do something more to protect myself besides using the stone. I looked hopefully toward the deserted island, wondering if I could swim to safety. But I realised it was too far to the shore and beyond my capability. I heard a noise close to me and froze with fear as I saw Robert's face appear level with the deck. It was flushed red with anger, his forehead beaded with sweat. Then like a raging bull he ascended the stairs, muttering insults as he went. I prayed again silently, my hand almost going into spasm as my grip tightened around the stone.

When he stood on the deck, he remained in one spot swaying for a moment, trying to focus and keep his balance at the same time. Then he staggered toward me, stopped and snarled, 'Are you frightened now?' With a surge of courage that surprised even myself, I took a step towards him and replied loudly with all the confidence I could muster; 'No'. To my surprise he backed away with such a look of shock on his face, it almost made me laugh despite the seriousness of the situation. He then retreated back down the ladder from whence he had come. I did not hear a sound from him again all night. If only he had realised that I was shaking so much that my knees were almost knocking together, despite my newfound courage. I sat down on the deck and gave thanks to God for providing me with a good dose of fearlessness, right when I needed it.

The next day we arrived in the Whitsundays and it was with great relief that I disembarked that yacht for the last time. During the trip, I was certain that Robert would harm me, if not kill me, as I would not succumb to his advances. I wrote a note for police to find should I come to harm and not return to my family. The note told all and revealed how I feared for my life. I placed it under the mattress in the cabin where I had only slept for the first week and a half. I have written an account of this mishap for you to read to show the consequences of doing life 'my way'. I have included two Proverbs from the Bible, one at the beginning and one at the end of this chapter, as they speak of the folly of following one's own will. I had no phone signal for most of the three weeks aboard the yacht, but thankfully, I had God's protection, even though I went on the trip despite feeling uncomfortable and not asking for His guidance. It was a huge lesson for me to pray to God about everything and seek His advice in the future. But God is patient and kind, and I was and still am a work in progress.

> *'Enthusiasm without knowledge is no good;*
> *haste makes mistakes'.*
> **—Proverbs 19:2 NLT—**

## Chapter Twenty-One

## *Revelation*

## —2012-2013—

As I watched my eldest granddaughter walk down the aisle on her wedding day, I recalled being at the hospital, awaiting the news of her birth. How quickly time had passed. I found myself reflecting on the impermanence of life. I thought about *my* childhood and the fact that I almost died when I was five days old. I wondered about the heavenly music I heard, as I sank into an unconscious state in our farm creek twelve years later and how I survived breast cancer twice. I realised during these brushes with death that God had been there with me. Why had He saved me? Was it because He wished for me to fulfil the plan He had for my life? I recalled the encounters I had with spirit beings while I was still incredibly young. I realised that they must have been satanic in nature. Why did that happen to me when I was an innocent child? There were so many unanswered questions.

Then I experienced another amazing encounter with God. A friend of mine invited me to a church meeting, and to be honest, I went along for no other reason except that I had nothing better to do that night. At this early stage in my Christian walk, my understanding was that once you asked Jesus to be your Lord and Saviour, there was not a lot more you had to do. And that there was nothing that needed to be added at the time you accept Jesus. I took the following scripture to mean exactly what it says. Colossians 2:9-10, the apostle Paul tells us; 'For in Him dwells all the fullness of the Godhead bodily; and you are complete in Him, who is the head of all principality and power'. I did not realise how much God yearns to have a personal relationship with us, and that each person's experience, once they have made this commitment, is different. At this particular church, the evangelist delivered his message then invited those who wished to give their lives to Jesus to come forward.

I felt excited as many people walked towards the front of the church and recalled the day I had accepted this same invitation. Then something very unusual happened. Suddenly *I* was walking forward. I noticed a battle happening in both my mind and body. In my mind I was thinking; 'What are you doing? This offer is for people who are accepting Jesus for the first time'. But my body persisted in moving forward. It was as though I was floating. I was very embarrassed, to say the least, and particularly concerned that there may be people I knew in this large crowd who were well aware that I had already invited Jesus to be my Lord and Saviour. What would they be thinking? Before I knew it, there I was, standing alongside many others, bewildered as to how and why I was there. The evangelist began praying for each person individually. When he stood before me, he placed his hands on my shoulders and prayed that I be baptised with the Holy Spirit. Immediately I sensed heat pass through my body like a powerful current. After the evangelist moved to the next person in line, I felt like I had been filled to overflowing with love, peace and joy. It was as though I had been refreshed and renewed spiritually.

A pastor came alongside me and explained that the Holy Spirit is a 'gift' God gave to all who believed in His Son when Jesus died and was raised again. And that the Holy Spirit would gently guide, comfort, gradually transform and restore me, to be the person God had originally created me to be. I was amazed to think that I had the Spirit of the living God who created the universe and raised Jesus from the dead living within me. This was new and important information that has since changed my life. In Romans 8:11, the apostle Paul tells us, 'But if the Spirit of Him who raised Jesus from the dead dwells in you, He who raised Christ from the dead will also give life to your mortal bodies through His Spirit who dwells in you'.

As I drove home that night, the love I felt from the gift of the Holy Spirit was overwhelming. I sang with sheer joy and told God how much I loved Him. I felt different. And hopefully, now with the Holy Spirit's guidance, I would not go on any more yacht trips or other adventures without first checking in with Him. I was beginning to understand the reason my friends had coped so well when they lost their baby not long after he was born. And why other Christian friends always prayed and asked God to help them when they needed to make major decisions, instead of relying on themselves to work things out. But as God also gives us free will as well as the Holy Spirit, it is then up to us to discern right from wrong. The Holy Spirit is a gentleman and will never force us to do anything. But whether or not we heed His guidance, or go our own way, is up to us.

After this event, it became very evident that the Holy Spirit was beginning to help me make sense of the mysteries contained in the Word of God. I was hungry and wanting to know more and more. So, I began spending every spare moment I had studying the Bible. In church I learned that God actually speaks to us through this precious book and guides us in the way He desires for us to live our lives on earth. God began to reveal Himself to me in a way I had never experienced previously.

I have heard it said before; 'What good is The Bible?' 'Man wrote it, not God'. I used to ask the very same question. I was now learning that God through the Holy Spirit, inspired forty authors to write sixty-six books of the Bible, over a period of 1,600 years. And the most incredible part of all is the fact that the message from each author was in total harmony, one with the other. The Bible is all about God's plan to save His children. We are His children. He is so passionate about us that He came to earth as Jesus in the flesh to deliver this good news to us. Psalm 119:105 tells us that God's Word (the Bible) is a lamp to our feet and a light to our path.

Jesus is alive and is working through believers' lives today, in the same way He did with His followers over 2,000 years ago. He does this through the power of the Holy Spirit. Why was this so hard for me to believe prior to inviting Jesus into my heart? I used to settle for superficial spirituality when I followed the New Age movement. I put my faith in fortune-tellers, palm readers, meditation, idols, rituals, 'the universe' and anyone or anything else that I so wrongly believed could show me the Truth I so desperately sought. None of this can be compared to Jesus. I now marvel at how faithful the prophets of old and the disciples of Jesus were, who received revelation directly from the Holy Spirit and wrote the most influential and powerful book of all time, the Bible.

## Chapter Twenty-Two

# *Reaching Out to the Lost*

## —2013—

I began attending church more regularly and after the sermon was delivered each Sunday, I often witnessed miraculous healings happening during the laying on of hands and prayer. Some folks who were healed were not yet walking with the Lord, just the same as when God first touched and healed me. But it was when they experienced His unconditional love for them, despite their unbelief, that many gave their lives to Jesus. These weren't just random one-off occurrences where people were caught up in some kind of 'group hysteria'. Some who were healed returned to the church with doctors' reports as evidence of the miracle God had performed in their lives.

I had no doubt now that what I was seeing was Jesus pouring out His love and compassion upon people. He has not changed since He performed many miracles with His disciples as witnesses, over 2,000 years ago. And today He desires to use us as His hands and feet, to share the Gospel message and pray for the sick. He can use anyone of any age to do this, so as to bring Glory to Himself. Some who are reading my book may not believe what I have witnessed and written in this chapter and the chapter following, and I totally understand. I am still in awe myself. But these events actually did take place.

When I began hearing the messages about Jesus, I realised that the desire I had as a small child to become a missionary had never left me. Back when I was four years old, I listened attentively as the minister at church spoke of little children just like me, dying of starvation all around the globe. (My mum often reminded my siblings and me of this, also, if we did not eat all the food she served us at mealtimes). The minister also told of how Jesus and His disciples had compassion for those less fortunate than themselves. Before Jesus was crucified, He told His disciples to go into all the world, preach the Gospel message so people would learn about Him; to lay hands on and pray for those afflicted with diseases and all manner of disabilities. Many people wandering aimlessly found direction and hope when they gave their life to Jesus. He sought justice for those mistreated by others, healing for the broken-hearted and comfort for those in mourning. Jesus did not come to condemn the world, but to save the world and set the captives free.

My prayer to God when I was a child went something like this: 'Please God, when I grow up, make a way so that I can go into the world, tell people about you and help the suffering, as Jesus did'.

I believe God places a desire within every human heart to seek Him and worship Him. Our lives are meant to be a love story. God created us to be in an intimate relationship with Him. This relationship is what I had been searching for so desperately but not realising at the time. I had felt that deep yearning and tried to fill it instead with relationships with men, alcohol, drugs and other counterfeit things. But we can never truly find fulfilment until we turn to God our Creator. But that is only the beginning. Until we allow Him to truly be our Lord and Saviour, we will never be complete. Once we come to God, we find who we really are. We are His children, the apple of His eye.

And now at the age of fifty-nine, I was praying once again that very same prayer I prayed so many years before: That I could somehow give hope to people in this broken world, especially those who had never been told about Jesus and His mighty Love for them. To have the chance to pray for the suffering, as I was beginning to do now in my own hometown. Our church sent out a team twice per year to deliver a message of Hope to people in far-off countries, where many had never heard about Jesus. I could not see a way for me to ever go with the team, as I struggled from week to week to simply support myself. I had no savings, but I knew that if I was meant to be Jesus' hands and feet whether in my own country or overseas, God would make a way.

I prayed to Him, 'Please God, use me in any way you want. I wish to serve You'.

I watched sadly each time the team from our church set out, dreaming that one day I would be able to go too.

In March 2013, Pastor Jack announced in church one Sunday that the team was going to Bulgaria, Macedonia, and possibly Israel in September of that year. He was asking for anyone who was interested to let him know. I was immediately on my knees. 'Please, God. Send me'. As I prayed, I tried my hardest to have faith in Him to provide the finances to make this possible. But only if it was His Will. Because my relationship with God was fairly new, I was very easily swayed by an overly critical internal voice pouring condemnation upon me with all barrels blazing. The voice went something like this: 'Who do you think you are? You have no experience and you are stupid'. But there was also another kind, soft, gentle voice assuring me that this time I was going.

The team went ahead and booked their flights. I kept praying, and as time went on, I became even more certain that I would be joining them despite the fact I had no spare money. But wait a minute. Yes, I did. It was in one of those light bulb moments that I remembered I had saved 3,000 Australian dollars in order to pay my taxes. But surely it would not be right for me to use that? If I spent that money, which I had earnestly set aside each week, how could I ever pay it back? I contacted my accountant and asked her when I would need to pay taxes that year. I was astonished when she informed me that it was not due until the following March.

I jumped, danced and rejoiced so much that I went weak in the knees. But then I began to have a few doubts. This was a huge venture. The team had booked three months previously. How would it be even possible that I could be on the same flights? And by now, did the pastor have enough volunteers already? But despite my doubts, I knew for certain that I was going on this trip and that it was definitely God's will for me. I phoned Mary and she was overjoyed to hear that I had found a way to come and assured me there was room for me. I prayed all the way to the travel centre and was amazed when the booking agent informed me that there was a seat available on every flight the team was on. By this time, I was almost dancing on the ceiling. I was not the least bit concerned about how I would save $3,000 to pay my tax in another six months. This was God's Will, so I put my trust in Him to work it out. Thankfully, I already had a passport

On the 18th of September 2013, I set out with the team from my local church headed up by Pastors Mary and Jack, on my very first trip to bring Hope to the lost and suffering. We flew from Rockhampton to Brisbane, Brisbane to Singapore; Singapore to Dubai, then on to Turkey where we stayed overnight. The next day we spent exploring the 'Grand Bazaar' markets and took a boat trip to the Asian side of Turkey. That evening we flew to Macedonia. We were picked up from the airport in Skopje and taken to a town called Stip, which is a large textile production centre, located in the Eastern part of Macedonia. We stayed in Stip for six days. I had no idea what lay ahead of me in the weeks to come. I was excited, to say the least, but nothing could have prepared me for how God moved.

Our host pastor in Macedonia was a mighty man of God, highly respected and loved amongst the congregations of the many churches he had planted. We drove with him and two or three of his 'disciples' who interpreted for us, from one church to another throughout the country. To say we had little rest, is an understatement. But to witness God's almighty love and compassion for his people, seemed to remove all weariness from us.

One afternoon after another busy day of visiting churches and praying for people, Pastor Jack informed us we had time for a quick shower prior to visiting a Gypsy church that evening. He told us to pray and ask God for a 'word of knowledge' as we prepared to leave, each in our own separate accommodation. I had never heard of such a thing. As I was showering, I asked God to reveal to me what a 'word of knowledge' was, in order that I could be prepared for the Church we were about to visit. Instantly, I saw visions in the form of small pictures, one after the other, moving slowly before my mind. It is hard to explain, except the pictures reminded me of old-fashioned photo negatives which were used in cameras in the 1970s and '80s in the form of a roll, that were developed into photos. These visions were of people of all ages, displaying disabilities of every form imaginable. This was all very new to me and the strangest thing was, I somehow knew all about each person's ailment. It was like an inner knowing, if that makes sense. I asked God to please stop showing me the visions until I finished showering. I wanted to write down what He was showing me in preparation for our pastor. Pastor Jack could then share these 'words of knowledge' with the church that evening.

After I was dressed and ready for the meeting, I carefully wrote a description of each vision, just as I had been shown by God. An example may be, 'older lady, itching skin', 'young man with broken leg that has never healed properly'. Then came the big ones. 'Cancer', 'brain tumour', 'stroke', 'blind from birth', 'deaf' and so on. I was guessing the ages of the people, according to how they appeared in each vision. Before I continue, I wish to explain that I took no pride in what God was revealing to me. I did not expect this to happen but was humbled by the fact that He was showing me these things. God loves us all and has no favourites. He can use anyone to do His will and often chooses 'the weak' and the 'broken' to serve Him.

We arrived at the church and pastor Jack enquired of the team, if any of us had a 'word of knowledge,' to which I replied in the affirmative. The service began with beautiful Christian Worship sung in the Macedonian native tongue. Some I recognized as songs we also sang in our church back home. Our pastor was then invited to come forward to preach the Gospel message, telling people about Jesus. After this, he called the team to the front of the church and introduced us, one at a time, through an interpreter. We had done this at every church we had visited thus far.

When we returned to our seats, pastor Jack explained to the congregation the process of 'laying on of hands', saying that God tells us in the Bible to do this to one another. He then gave the 'words of knowledge' he had received, and people with those ailments, came forward for prayer. Next thing he was inviting me to the front, explaining to the congregation that I also had some 'words'. I was in shock that he would ask me to do this. I thought that I would just hand him the list I had written and he would read it out. I immediately moved from belief in what God had shown me to 'disbelief'. It seemed I did not have a choice except to come to the front of the church and deliver the messages I thought I had received from Him.

God had shown me in one of the visions a lady suffering with tremors in her head and face. I spoke this 'word' and a woman came forward. Imagine my shock when after prayer, she began jumping around, crying. I thought maybe something had gone terribly wrong and that I had somehow caused her condition to worsen. The interpreter finally calmed her enough to ask her how she was feeling, and she said that the tremors she had had for years were now completely gone. What I needed to understand was that the healing of this lady had nothing to do with me. It was Jesus who healed her. Once I remembered this, it was as though a burden shifted from me. My responsibility was to obey Him by speaking out the 'words' He had given to me, laying hands on the afflicted and praying for them to be healed in His Mighty Name. Then it was up to Him.

That night we witnessed many more miracles. It was amazing to experience Jesus healing people through us and at times feeling physical symptoms suddenly alter as we prayed. For example, one man suffered tight hamstrings which made it extremely painful for him to walk. When I placed my hands on the backs of his legs and prayed for him, he told me he felt incredible warmth come into his legs and the tension loosen immediately. It was both miraculous and humbling to see people who had suffered pain for many years in different areas of their bodies set free at last.

When God first gave me 'words of knowledge', He showed me a vision of a small gypsy girl. I guessed that she was approximately eighteen months old. God revealed to me that she had suffered from a problem in her right hip since birth, causing her leg to turn outwards, making it impossible for her to walk. We had been to many churches in two days, and each time I spoke out the 'word' concerning this small girl, no one came forward. I began to have great doubts about my ability to hear from God. Pastor Jack encouraged me not to lose heart and to believe what I had heard. I had already spoken this 'word' at least six times and found myself searching for this small child amongst the crowd in each church we visited. Then I heard God's voice speak to me and say, 'Have faith in me. Believe what I have told you. You will have the opportunity to pray for her soon'.

In each church we visited, immediately following the Gospel

message our pastor called me forward to give 'words' I had heard from God. I spoke the most recent ones then repeated the 'word' God had given me, for the little girl. One night after I had spoken of this child, some people toward the back of the church became excited and very vocal as they conversed with one another. I asked the interpreter what all the fuss was about, and he said that they knew the child and she would be at the meeting in the church we were visiting the next evening. Hope rose within me once again. The next night I was so excited at the prospect of praying for this precious little one that I began to look around for her once again. But then I recalled the words God spoke to me the previous night. 'Have Faith in me. Believe what I have told you'.

When Pastor Jack called me forward and I faced the congregation, I could not help but notice the young girl was not present, but I spoke the 'word' regardless. I was trembling. I knew I had heard from God and I believed He would somehow bring her to us so He could heal her. But where was she? I placed my little book I kept especially for 'words of knowledge', reluctantly back into my bag. It was then I noticed a young lady walking towards me. As she came closer, I realised she was crying. The interpreter spoke to her briefly, then explained that this was the child's mother, and for some reason, she was not able to bring her little one to the meeting.

The distraught mum clung to me and sobbed. I just held her, and when she lifted her head and looked at me, I noticed my shirt was wet from her tears. I asked the interpreter to tell her that we could pray for her child regardless and would anoint a handkerchief with oil and pray over it so she could take it and place it directly on the child, in her clothing, or under her pillow. I had witnessed our pastor do this back home and had heard many good reports of miraculous healings taking place as a result. The team and I prayed with her for God to miraculously touch her little one and heal her, but then I watched as she left the church, my heart heavy that I didn't get the opportunity to pray for her little girl in person. Whatever happened now though, I was certain God was going to heal her so she could walk for the very first time in her life.

After we finished praying for many others, I sat down on a seat feeling exhausted. A sudden movement at the back of the church caused me to turn around. To my shock, I saw the mum whom I had prayed with walking towards me carrying a sleeping child. As she approached, I realised without any doubt at all that this was the little one God had shown me in the vision. I began experiencing a mixture of emotions of excitement, insecurity, unbelief, fear and doubt. Once again, the voice in my head questioned me, 'Did you really hear from God?' As I motioned for the mother to sit on a chair with the little one on her knee, a crowd of relatives and friends of this family came and stood behind her. They appeared to be in eager anticipation of what was about to take place. It was then that I began to relax. There was no expectation of what *I* was going to do. I could not heal a big toe. The expectation was solely on God, and it was His business what He did in this situation.

Little did I know that I was about to experience the miracle that changed my mind dramatically about who God is and what He is capable of doing through others to bring Glory to Himself. I looked to Mary to help. In some way, I guess I was hoping to give God the opportunity to change His mind about using me. After all, she was experienced at praying and the laying on of hands. She and Jack had been doing it for years. Maybe any minute now she would step in and take over. But it wasn't to be. Instead, she picked up her iPad in preparation to discreetly take some photos. I silently prayed a desperate plea to God, and a very small 'voice' said, 'Trust Me. Have Faith in Me'.

I asked the interpreter to seek permission from the mother for me to pray for her child. The mother simply nodded her head and smiled at me in agreement. I knelt before them. The little girl was awake now, and her big brown gypsy eyes were full of fear. She edged herself even higher up on her mother's lap, scrambling backwards so as to be as far away from me as she could possibly get.

I glanced at Mary with a quizzical look, as if to say, 'What now'? She mouthed silently to me to pray for the spirit of fear to leave the small child. I did as she suggested. When I finished praying and opened my eyes, the previously terrified, brown-eyed Gypsy child was smiling at me.

My heart melted. She appeared to be totally relaxed now. It was very obvious that God had removed all of her fear. I tentatively, placed one of my hands on the little girl's ankle and one on her hip. My prayer was simple. I asked Jesus to heal her and demanded the infirmity to go in His mighty name. I felt her foot turn slightly. I opened my eyes and Mary confirmed this had, in fact, happened, by showing me with her thumb and forefinger a measurement of approximately three quarters of an inch.

The relatives and the child's mother had all witnessed this and were rejoicing. I prayed again, and this time there was a dramatic movement in both hip and foot. After I prayed again for the third time, I felt a 'click' beneath the hand I had placed on her hip. When I opened my eyes, I was not surprised to see that the little girl's foot and leg were back in place. The power of God coming through my body into that little child was like electricity going through a transformer. I was in absolute awe. The family was dumb-struck. When people witness the power of God for the first time, their lives are often never quite the same again. A greater relationship with God is often their desire. This is exactly how I felt right now.

I requested that the mother stand her little girl on the floor. God had told me He would heal her so she could walk and not only walk but run. The mum was very reluctant. With the help of the interpreter she explained that doctors and physiotherapists had told her that her daughter would never be able to put weight on her leg, let alone stand up. She said she was happy that her little girl looked normal now. It was as though she was not willing to risk undoing the miracle Jesus had already performed. This was when Mary took charge of the situation. Stepping forward, she boldly took the small child from the safe haven of her mother's lap and stood her on the floor. The little one pushed herself upwards until both of her legs were straight. Mary encouraged the mother to take one of her little girl's hands, while she took the other. There were audible gasps of disbelief as the small girl walked the length of the church and then ran back to where I was standing.

This is The Power of God. The church team still travels and ministers in Eastern Europe annually, returning with photos and videos of this little girl, five years on, running and playing as God intended her to. In the latest video, there was a testimony from her mother explaining how God had healed her child, four years previously, after she received prayer. This was no coincidence. It was not a random one-off healing that occurred one night somewhere in a church in Macedonia. When people are in disbelief about Jesus still healing today, I look at the video evidence on my iPhone of this little one and the testimony from her mother. I Praise God that He used me as a vessel to bring His Love and Healing to her. I also thank Him for the healing this brought about in my own life – I was healed of disbelief and doubt about God's mighty power.

I was very encouraged by this whole trip. The team and I witnessed many people giving their lives to Jesus and God bringing an end to their suffering. But not all were healed. Not while we were present, at least. Quite often, when the team returned to these countries the following year, they were told of miracles happening in the weeks following prayer. God is mighty and Sovereign and may His Will be done. We continued praying for people in different churches throughout Macedonia.

It was a privilege to spend one day in a village for which our church in Australia had provided financial support. The latest project that had been completed was a pipeline from a water source to the village for the residents who were both Muslim and Christian. Before the pipeline was put in place, the people used to walk four hours to obtain enough water to provide for their family's needs each day. When we first arrived, we noticed a sign hanging over a holding tank, and on the sign was written 'Jesus water'. Our donation was also used to purchase goats. It filled my heart with joy to see the goats, some with kids, grazing on lush green pasture. A couple of the residents told us that the land had been barren prior to the pipeline. The goats and their 'kids' were a source of milk, cheese and meat for all of the people in the village.

Our host pastor took the team to show us the progress being made on a church he was having built in this same village. Prior to our arrival that day, God had shown me a vision of a woman. In the vision she was holding her forearm, obviously in great pain. The Lord told me she had suffered with the injury for four years. To my amazement, as we approached the main entrance to the church, I noticed two elderly ladies in a squatted posture, chatting to one another. As we drew closer, I immediately recognised one of them as the lady God had shown me. She was dressed in black with a shawl draped over her head and was cradling one of her forearms protectively. I asked an interpreter to ask the lady if I could pray for her. She was obviously happy about my request, as she gave me a toothless grin and carefully rose to her feet.

When she presented her arm to me, it was so badly broken that it looked as though one of the bones had crossed over the other. I asked the interpreter to ask her how long she had suffered with this terrible injury.

I was in awe of God when she replied, 'About four years'.

I prayed to Him to take all pain from this woman and bring healing to her forearm, in Jesus' Name. God answered my prayer. The old lady began leaping in delight as the pain she had lived with for four years left her body completely. She regained full movement and became so wildly excited, pumping her arm back and forth, that I was afraid she may cause herself a strain of some sort. The residents of this village and surrounding areas are very poor and have no means of transport to go to hospital if the need arises. The hospitals often charge money for those seeking medical assistance and for any ongoing care.

I did not go on this trip seeking 'signs and wonders'. That was not my desire, even as a four-year-old child. Jesus and his disciples always put others before themselves, and He also wants *us* to do this. They brought the Good News of the Gospel to the people, then set about comforting the broken-hearted, praying for the sick and giving hope to the lost. Jesus had compassion and love for all who were in need, no matter the reason. This trip for me, personally, was definitely about bringing the Gospel and His Healing to the suffering, but it was also about God revealing Himself to me. I believe He was showing me that there was a different way. That I could return to that childhood desire, humbling myself before Him, serving Him and making it become a reality. This was all about having a heart for others in any situation and wherever I may be. Being Jesus' hands and feet by trying to always look out for whoever is in front of me, and to grow closer and closer to God every day, becoming more aware of His Will and not my own. I want Him to use me to bring Glory to Himself. What an honour and privilege to serve Him.

## Chapter Twenty-Three

# *They Will Lay Hands on the Sick*

### —2013-2014—

*'They will lay hands on the sick, and they will recover'.*

— Mark 16:18—

On the 25th September 2013, the team returned to Stip. We had been greatly encouraged by our host pastor as he took us to visit each church he had planted throughout Macedonia. It was obvious that he played a big part in people's lives being transformed by Jesus due to his obedience and faith in God. We were truly privileged to see the fruit of the work he had so faithfully been doing for several years now.

We were relieved when Pastor Jack informed us we could take a day to rest. I was so grateful for this time in order to absorb and reflect on all that had taken place on our journey so far. I was in awe of God's unconditional love toward every person, even though most had previously turned away from Him. I witnessed people being set free as they were introduced to Jesus through the power of the Gospel message, and after that, the laying on of hands. They were free at last from physical ailments and the emotional and spiritual burdens of darkness that had previously bound them, preventing them from having a relationship with God. Even though I had seen these same miracles in our church in Australia, I was still in awe. As I rested, I reflected on how God had made it possible for me to be part of the team on this trip. I had pleaded with Him for three years to make a way for me to be able to come. It was in His perfect timing and I know that if I had tried to rush ahead of Him, I would not have been equipped for what I was experiencing now.

One of the things God was teaching me was how to have faith in Him, no matter what the circumstances of my life might look like.

Most of the people we met in Eastern Europe lived in poverty, relying totally on God to provide for all their needs. I noticed many used donkeys as their mode of transport and to carry heavy loads. It was like stepping back in time. I saw shepherds watching over their flocks, still using a shepherd's crook, just like the pictures on a Christmas card. The winter is very harsh in this region and one of the disciples we were travelling with told us how he took his donkey into the forest to gather firewood to keep his family from perishing in the cold. I reflected on how Jesus helped the poor and the lost and how God tells us in His Word that we are to also look out for the needs of widows and orphans. We witnessed this in a church in Macedonia where there was a very primitive kitchen with a huge stone oven, used specifically to bake hundreds of loaves of bread each week for orphans and widows.

After spending some time in Stip, we moved to Bulgaria and were hosted by another wonderful pastor and his wife. We continued watching in amazement as the Gospel message was preached with many giving their lives to Jesus. God continued to move through us as we prayed and laid hands on people, resulting in mighty signs and wonders. As we saw and felt His love and compassion for those who were suffering, our Faith soared higher and higher as we grew very humble in our ministry and love for Jesus. 'Words of knowledge', brought people forward with all kinds of infirmities. Some of these were: Repeating one's self over and over, memory loss (dementia), tremors, depression from a broken heart, (this lady left the meeting filled with the Joy of The Lord), severe headaches, pain in the rib cage, scoliosis causing immense pain, hearing loss, visual impairments, tumours, back pain, emotional problems, knee problems, hip problems, bowel, bladder, liver and heart problems, diabetes, neck pain, ankle pain, infection, itching skin and more.

Most were healed immediately. One man who had been lame from birth leapt and danced after prayer. Most people with pain in their bodies walked out of the meetings pain free. One blind man said that he could see shadows now. I told him I believed God had begun a work in him and He would finish it. Tremors disappeared before our eyes, kyphosis (curvature of the spine), healed so those affected were able to stand upright once again, palpable tumours disappeared. Movement was restored to body parts where there had been no movement sometimes for years. Hearing restored fully and sadness replaced with Joy. Some people came to the church to ask us to pray for relatives or friends with particular problems who lived too far away to attend the meetings, or in some circumstances were too ill to travel. In these cases, we anointed handkerchiefs with oil, prayed over them and gave them to the friend or relative to pass on to the person with the ailment. The afflicted person then placed the anointed handkerchief on their body so Jesus could heal them. The Apostle Paul speaks of this in the book of Acts, 19:12.

On the fourth of October 2013, we flew from Sofia in Bulgaria to Istanbul, then on to Israel. This was yet another dream come true for me – to visit The Holy Land where Jesus was born, ministered to the people and was then crucified. We were fortunate to have as our tour guides a relative of Pastor Jack's and his 'Messianic Jewish' wife. They were a lovely, humble couple. Among some of the places they took us to visit was Mount Megiddo. (Tel Megiddo). The city of Megiddo has not existed since the Persian invasion about 2,300 years ago. There are some remarkably interesting ruins there including what is thought to be actual stables and mangers King Solomon used for his horses. The ruins are the remains of what used to be a military centre during the King's reign. Megiddo is known for its theological importance by its Greek name 'Armageddon'. The book of Revelation (the last book of the Bible), prophetically states that Armageddon is the place where the last great battle will be fought, when the forces of good (Jesus Christ and His Heavenly army) will triumph over evil (Satan and his demonic forces).

Our first accommodation in Israel was located twenty minutes east of Nazareth and west of Haifa at a place called Beit Lechem Ha Gililt, meaning 'Bethlehem of Galilee'. I took great delight in rising early in the morning and picking pomegranates to eat before breakfast. Another place we visited was Mount Carmel where Baal and Elijah met to prove whose God was real (1 Kings 18:22-40). Then one Saturday, the team and I had the privilege of attending a Messianic Jewish church Service. It was a wonderful experience and our pastors were invited to minister there. We were told by some of the congregation that because their church is located in the valley of Megiddo, some believe it is cursed.

We visited Caesarea and saw the ruins of King Herod The Great's Palace. This was his beach retreat where he took time out and entertained guests. For me, Jerusalem was the highlight of our tour of Israel. Our Jewish friends suggested we hire a guide who was more familiar with the area and its history. The guide took us to the City of David, where we saw the Siloam Pool where Jesus healed the blind man. We walked through a tunnel under Jerusalem and through Hezekiah's tunnel which he built to bring water from one side of the city to the other. We saw the supposed ruins of King David's Palace and where Bathsheba was bathing when the King summoned for her to come to him (2 Samuel 11.) It was a little difficult to access the Wailing Wall, as there were huge crowds waiting their turn. However, my patience paid off and I eventually managed to pray and tuck my handwritten prayer into a crevice in the wall. We went to Mount Zion and the Mount of Olives and walked the 'Dolorosa Street' in the Old City of Jerusalem, believed to be the path Jesus walked on the way to his crucifixion. This was a very moving experience.

Among other amazing places we visited was The Mount of Beatitudes where Jesus delivered the 'Sermon on the Mount'. Here we sat under a tree, and our friend and guide read from the Bible Mathew 5:3-12, 'The Beatitudes', which means Blessings. We visited Capernaum where Jesus taught with His disciples. People back then were amazed at what He told them, as He did so with such authority, which was different to what they were used to hearing from their teachers of the law. Some of our touring took us close to the borders, and we were reminded by our friends and guides how the surrounding countries are enemies of Israel.

We moved on to Tiberias and stayed in accommodation overlooking the Sea of Galilee. One very memorable moonlit night, we were given the opportunity to learn traditional Israeli Folk Dancing on a deck overlooking the moon-drenched water. I thought of Jesus and His disciples ministering to the people here and crossing by boat from one side of the lake to the other, often trying to rest from the crowds. I recalled from the Bible how Jesus walked on the Sea of Galilee to His disciples who were in a boat being tossed to and fro at the mercy of the huge waves. And how He called Peter, one of His disciples, to trust Him to leave the boat and walk to Him on the water. You can read this account in Mathew 14:22-33.

The story is about how, while Peter kept His eyes on Jesus and trusted in Him, he stayed afloat. But once he looked at the circumstances surrounding them both, he began to sink and called out to Jesus to save him from certain death. What a great reminder this is for me when I feel as though I am 'drowning' at times in my circumstances. There was a mountain behind our accommodation and as I walked one morning, I imagined that maybe that was where Jesus went to pray the night before He deeply disturbed His disciples by His miraculous act of walking on water. I did not wish to leave Israel, wanting to stay longer to soak up the history of the time of Jesus ministry and life there. But, sadly, we had to depart.

One day not long after arriving home from this amazing trip, I was sitting next to Mary in church, when Pastor Jack announced that a team would be leaving in late December for Bali, West Timor, Java and Roti Island, to bring the Word of God to the people there and to pray for those who were suffering. I immediately felt a gentle nudge in my side and turned as Mary whispered to me, 'You are going on this trip'. I almost laughed and whispered a reply to her, 'You haven't seen my bank balance'. I knew it was close to zero. And I was very aware that I still needed to save the three thousand dollars that I owed for my tax as I had previously spent the allotted amount on my trip.

That night as I tried to sleep, I was deeply troubled. I tossed and turned and kept waking to a gentle voice in my head repeating the word 'Indonesia'. The voice became so persistent that I turned on the light and tried to read, but the distraction of this repetitive voice was so great, I could not concentrate. Eventually, I fell into a deep sleep, and when I woke in the morning, I discovered an unusual message on my phone. It was from a work colleague whom I had not seen or heard from in at least six years. She was messaging to ask if I was interested in selling her a therapeutic aid I had purchased ten years earlier to use as an extra tool for my work in remedial massage. I had put the aid in a drawer and had promptly forgotten about it after using it once or twice and finding it of no benefit. My colleague was offering a very reasonable price for this long-forgotten item, and within hours she came to my home to complete the sale, paying me in cash.

As she drove away, I glanced at the money in my hand and remembered the gentle 'voice' I had heard the previous night. It suddenly dawned on me that I was holding half the amount of the fare for the trip to Indonesia. And, to my surprise, the remainder of the money required was in my bank account by the end of that week. Some wonderful friends of mine who are like family to me were obedient to God when He spoke to them about paying for the balance of my airfare. I then realised that this was once again God's will, and I needed to be obedient to Him no matter how strange the request may have seemed. Mary and Jack were not at all surprised when I contacted them and told them I was able to accompany them on the next trip. Two months later we arrived in Indonesia.

Once again, I witnessed God's mighty Love and Compassion for humanity. Many gave their lives to Jesus and were healed in His Name, and my faith in Him soared to yet another level. But, once again, not all gave their lives to Jesus and not all were healed. God works in mysterious ways, and who are we to question? Not everyone was healed when Jesus was on earth and many also rejected the Gospel message back then. Often it is only in our weakness that we really seek Him and depend on Him.

I recall visiting a village in the mountains where many people gathered for a meeting. Some attended out of curiosity, but others were in desperate need of a touch from God. After the Gospel message, thirty-four people gave their lives to Jesus. Pastor Jack then invited people to come forward who needed prayer, and many with all kinds of infirmities accepted the invitation. One man had suffered a stroke seven years previously. He was in a wheelchair, head slumped forward and paralysed down one entire side of his body. Hence, he could not walk or raise the effected arm. After we prayed for him a couple of times, we noticed no dramatic change except that he told us through an interpreter, that he now had feeling in the affected side of his body. We prayed once more, believing that the man was completely healed and thanked God ahead of time for answering our prayers.

One week later while we were still in Indonesia, we received a phone call telling us the great news that God had answered our prayer for the man who had the stroke and was of the Muslim Faith. He no longer needed the assistance of his wheelchair and was walking around the village for the first time in seven years. The entire community recognised him and were shocked to see his changed condition.

When they enquired of him how could this be, he simply replied, 'A man named Jesus healed me'.

What a testimony. All Glory be to God for this miracle.

Pastor's Mary and Jack had donated money to the local church in this village, and we received good news when we returned home that all of those who had given their lives to Jesus that day had received a Bible and were eagerly studying the Scriptures and enjoying their freedom in Christ.

On Roti Island we had the opportunity to witness twenty people in one night accept Jesus after hearing the Gospel and receiving prayer. Many were healed of such conditions as tuberculosis (followed up by doctor's report confirming this), and other breathing conditions. A small child who was lame due to polio walked for the first time.

One morning while visiting Kupang, a male member of our team and I were sharing breakfast with a pastor from Bali when she made a very strange request. She told us that her sister had been diagnosed with breast cancer via a biopsy and that she was scheduled to have a mastectomy in a few weeks. She informed my friend and me that her sister was currently at her workplace in Jakarta and between the two of them, they had arranged for us to pray for her, via speakerphone. When the pastor's sister received our call, she excused herself from her workstation and went to the bathroom. We prayed two or three times for Jesus to heal her completely of breast cancer. The sister placed her hand over the palpable tumour in her breast as we prayed and told us that with each prayer, the tumour became smaller until, finally, she could no longer feel it. We praised the Lord together, and within three weeks we received the great news that prior to the scheduled operation, the sister had advised the surgeon that she could no longer physically feel the tumour. Upon examination, he decided to run further tests. The results clearly revealed that there was no longer a tumour in her breast. God takes my breath away. He is indescribable.

We then visited a rehabilitation centre for those recovering from drug and alcohol abuse and witnessed many being touched and set free through the power and love of Jesus. Pastor Mary and Jack had visited a Sudanese village the previous year and prayed for many of the Muslim faith, who were healed. The resident pastors were frightened in case this caused unrest among the people over what had taken place. Early next morning they heard someone knocking on their door and they feared for their lives.

This was until they listened amazed as a crowd outside asked, 'Where are the Christian pastors from Australia who prayed for some of our people yesterday? We want them to pray for us also, as many of our friends and family were healed'.

So here we were, twelve months later at the local pastor's house, listening attentively as he recounted the story of what had taken place the previous year. As he finished speaking, there came a knock at the door and then our team experienced almost exactly what had taken place the year before. This is what I wrote in my diary on the day we visited this village:

'Every person who came to the pastor's house for healing was of the Muslim faith. They told us they had come because they were ailing and wanted prayer so Jesus would heal them. That day, every person we prayed for was healed, and we had the opportunity to tell them more about Jesus. Some of the infirmities they had were paralysis down one side from stroke, gout, hip pain, back pain, knee problems and a broken wrist. One lady asked for prayer, explaining that prior to the healing she had received the previous year, she had been so severely affected with Parkinson's disease she was unable to sleep at night. Since receiving prayer, all shaking had ceased. But this year, she thought she had felt a slight tremor and wished to be touched by Jesus again, to make sure her condition did not return'.

I was thinking that God could not do anything more to bring me to my knees when we were given the privilege to stay in an orphanage in Bali. I love children as they bring the serious adult side of me to an abrupt standstill, helping me to be free and childlike for a time. We arrived at the orphanage in the late afternoon and received such a warm welcome from the children that it bought tears to my eyes. The older girls prepared a meal for us and then all of the children sang a thanksgiving song, first in English, then Balinese. The pastors who take care of the orphans are a husband and wife team, along with the help of a few volunteers.

I thanked them for the meal, and one of the pastors explained to me that they do not always have food to eat. In fact, the children often go to bed hungry and attend school the next day regardless. This broke my heart. She went on to tell me of a time not so long ago when they went without food for three days. On the evening of the third day, God told the pastor He was going to provide for the children that night. She knew she had heard from God, so she told her husband to ask the children to set the table and sing thanksgiving songs to the Lord, just as they normally did each evening before their meal. In the meantime, she returned to their house across the courtyard to pray.

She fell to her knees before God, pleading with Him to provide for them, believing that He was going to do so. She thanked Him for His provision, and as soon as she finished praying, she heard a knock on her door. When she opened it, there was a man with a very puzzled look on his face. He told the lady that he was on his way to market when his cart overturned in the lane out in front of the orphanage. The entire contents of fresh fruit and vegetables were now bruised and scattered all over the road. He asked if she knew of anyone who would be able to use this produce as he could no longer sell it. This was not an unusual occurrence in the lives of the orphans and their carers. They relied on God to provide for them daily.

As I listened to story after story of how the children came to be in the orphanage, I was in awe of how God used people and their circumstances to rescue them, giving them a future and a hope. There were three brothers, all under the age of seven, originally from a small island quite a distance from Bali. Their parents were extremely poor and grew their own produce to feed their family. They had recently experienced a severe drought, which caused their supply of food to run out, leaving them with nothing to sustain them. The parents realised the terrible fate they were facing and decided to give their children a chance to survive. They placed them into a small wooden boat and pushed it as far as they could into the ocean. Their hope was that someone would find their boys somehow, or that the boat would wash up on land, and that someone would discover their children and take care of them.

Miraculously, the three young brothers were discovered by police three days later, not far off the coast of Bali, and were taken to the orphanage. One can only imagine the suffering and trauma their parents endured as they slowly starved to death, not knowing whether their precious children had been rescued. Even though the little boys had recovered physically from their exposure to the elements whilst at sea, I felt sad when I tried to imagine the trauma they must have experienced as they drifted alone for three days and nights, oblivious to what their future held.

Another little boy who had recently come to live at the orphanage was found abandoned on a busy street in Bali. He looked as though he was around two years old and had lumps from insect bites all over his little face and head. He began to sit at my feet as we sang worship songs and prayed. Each night he edged his way closer to me, until one evening he rested his back against my leg. I reached down and placed my hand on his small shoulder. At first, he moved away, but gradually his trust grew enough to allow me to rest my hand there as I prayed for him. I could not comprehend the fear and uncertainty he must have suffered. But I was so grateful that he had been rescued and bought to this place that was full of God's love, compassion and healing.

I marvelled as I watched the children creating their own games, using whatever was at hand. They often pushed plastic chairs around, pretending they were cars or used pieces of wood to create other games. The girls loved to swing and play on a rusty old swing set that had been donated to the orphanage. The chorus of children singing as they went about their morning chores before school woke me each day. One morning I heard a little girl singing like a lark in the courtyard below. I went to the window and discovered it was Rosie, a three-year-old bundle of sheer joy and mischief all rolled into one. She was sweeping the front entry way and stairs with a little straw broom. All of a sudden, her sweet melody ceased, and she raced down the stairs and pointed her little broom at two small boys. She reprimanded them for some reason or another, then burst into song once more, resuming the task at hand. All of the children five years and over attended school, some even managing to further their education at university.

At the end of this trip, I realised I was now better prepared to return home and continue God's will for me in my own country. For a while, at least. As I draw from the information I wrote in my diary at the time this was all taking place, I am so thankful that I documented significant events as they were happening. I am eternally grateful to pastors Mary and Jack for becoming my friends and for encouraging me to be part of the team. This profoundly changed my life. What I have written in this chapter and the one previous may be controversial to some, but these events actually did take place.

I managed to pay my tax back by the due date, then something else extremely exciting occurred. My eldest granddaughter and her husband became the proud parents of a baby boy, and then another, a couple of years later. I could hardly believe that my eldest daughter was now a grandmother, and I had become a great grandmother.

## Chapter Twenty-Four

## How I Found My Son

### —1970-2016—

*'To everything there is a season,
A time for every purpose under heaven'.*

—Ecclesiastes 3:1—

All things are in the hand of God who makes everything happen in the time He judges appropriate. This chapter shares the events that took place over a period of forty-six and a half years that finally made a way for my son and me to meet for the first time since his birth in 1970.

My daughters were anxious to find their brother and began searching many different avenues. Even though my four girls had not spent time with him, they somehow felt connected. We always spoke of my son as being family and we all looked forward to the day we would finally meet him. In chapter fifteen, I explained how the Australian Government changed a law in 1988, giving birth mothers access to their adopted children's birth certificates. I also mentioned how, after obtaining my son's birth certificate, I was informed that he did not know he was adopted, so any hope I had of meeting him was put on hold for the time being.

The Internet became publicly available in 1991, and I watched in awe as my second eldest daughter searched and found her brother. She also discovered where he was living at the time. Even though I was overjoyed by this information, I had no intention of interrupting his life. I just wanted to know that he was safe and well. Words cannot describe how valuable this small skerrick of news about him was to me, and after all this time I was content with this. It was the first glimmer of hope I had in twenty-one years, and I held it closely to my heart as though I feared that somehow it would be snatched from me.

A couple of years later, a friend mentioned that I should try to find out a little more about my son by contacting his place of employment. After thinking on this a while, I decided to take her advice, phone his work and hopefully speak with someone in charge who knew him. I did not want my inquiry to cause him any grief, so I was trying to be incredibly careful with my approach. I am not at liberty to reveal any details of the phone conversation that followed, as it is a private matter, except to say that the outcome of the phone call was that my son found out that he was adopted. I was very upset to say the least. I did not intend to hurt him in any way and regretted making the call. For many months, guilt consumed me. I had waited so long to find out if he was alright and now I felt that I had rushed things in my desire to know more about him. I still hoped and prayed that we would meet one day but thought it was best to let things settle a while before we tried to contact him again.

Twelve months later, my girls decided they had waited long enough. They wanted to meet their brother. I wasn't sure how I felt about this. For the past twenty-six years, I had longed to meet him also, but I had remained sensitive to his situation. I was still very conscious that through our yearning to meet him, we may disrupt his life which could have a detrimental effect on his emotional well-being. But my second eldest daughter talked to me about it, and I finally agreed to accompany her to a phone booth for her to call and introduce herself to him. I could see that she was almost as nervous about this as I was. Her hand trembled as she tentatively placed some coins into the pay phone and dialled my son's work number. I could not stop shaking and tried to hold myself together by leaning on the glass at the back of the phone booth.

Before long, I realised my daughter was talking to her brother and explaining to him who she was. I listened as she answered questions he was obviously asking her. Before long I saw her visibly relaxing as she laughed and chatted with him for what seemed like an eternity. I remained glued to the phone booth wall, still shaking as tears of joy poured from my eyes in an uncontrollable stream.

Then I heard my daughter say, 'I will put her on the phone'.

I was shocked and motioned to her that I was too overcome to speak. After all these years, the fact that my son would even want to have anything to do with me was a little too much to take in. Even though he did not know the real story behind his adoption, I expected him to reject me. Obviously, I was still carrying the scars of torment and the labels other people had put on me, as well as the ones I had put on myself. It was like I was branded with those names, and they were etched into my skin for all the world to see.

About three weeks later, I plucked up the courage and phoned my son. I cannot describe the different emotions I experienced when I heard his voice for the very first time. We gradually got to know each other via phone calls over the months that followed, and discovered that we had much in common, even though he had grown up with another family. I treasured every call and especially the one when he told me that he had three children; two girls and a boy. My heart felt as though it was about to burst wide open. I longed to know them as well, but I restrained my emotional longing and yearning, being mindful that my son had grown up with his adoptive mother and father, and that these children whom I considered to be my grandchildren, already had grandparents, who, I was sure, loved them very much. I did not wish to lose any of them by being 'over the top'. I held myself together during our phone conversations, but once I had hung up the receiver, I cried with joy and danced with happiness, over my beautiful once lost, now found family. Then, due to unfortunate circumstances, we had to break contact for many years. This was neither my son's nor my choice.

Approximately four years later I consented to share my story with a local newspaper about my personal journey as a birth mother. This was just prior to an apology made by the government on behalf of the nation of Australia to acknowledge the trauma of forced adoption on birth mothers over several decades. The journalist sat on my front veranda asking questions and recording what I had experienced while living in the home for unmarried mothers and how my baby was taken from me at birth. I could tell she was good at her job as she attempted to extract from me the drama she so hoped to record for the newspaper article as a pre-cursor to the 'apology'. She asked if I was still angry due to the ill treatment I had endured. How did I feel about it now, after all these years? She was very taken aback by my reply.

I told her that I had changed my mind about a lot of things. When she prompted me to explain what I meant, I told her the truth. I had realised in recent years that I had given a couple who were unable to have a child of their own the gift of my son. And not only that, I knew for certain that I was going to meet him one day, as I had been praying to God about this. The reporters face fell, and she replied, 'But it was so wrong. What about the terrible treatment you received in hospital'?

I then went on to explain to her that I had been presented with the most wonderful opportunity to forgive the very person who had caused me so much pain and shame, when I returned to the same hospital twelve years later to give birth to my third daughter. The very same midwife who had delivered my son also delivered my daughter and asked me to forgive her for the shameful way she had treated me.

This was obviously not the ending to the story the reporter had come to extract from me. She was not expecting (neither was she wanting) a 'happy ever after' kind of story. She packed up her things and left my home. My story was published in the paper; minus the wonderful events I had told her of at the end. So, in essence, the story in the newspaper made no sense at all and was no longer my story, which was one of love and hope.

After speaking to the reporter, the desire to meet my son became almost overwhelming. In December 2015, I took a chance and phoned him. As we talked and caught up on each other's news, it was as though we had never lost contact. He spoke of some extremely hard times he had been through, talked about his children and told me that he had met a lovely lady. I was overcome with joy as I told my daughters later that day, word for word almost, of our phone conversation. Normally I would have felt undeserving, but not anymore. I knew God's hand was in this situation and therefore, the end result would be out of this world.

Pieces of the puzzle of my life seemed to be fitting together now. Once again, I was reminded of the goodness of God and I knew for the first time that I had a destiny. There was hope. I desired to know God more intimately. His goodness in this situation was overtaking me, making it almost too much for me to understand why He would bother with little old me. I was a dirty rotten sinner who had done nothing but run from Him my entire life. Now I could feel that He was beginning to heal me and to fill the inner void that had been there since I was a little girl. All my life, I had tried to supplant that emptiness in dysfunctional and meaningless ways. I felt drawn to spend more time with Him, so I began in earnest to read His Word and meditate on what I was reading. It seemed to me that I was changing. I worried less, slept peacefully at night for the first time in many years, and had God to lean on in times of trouble. I realised I was happier than I had ever been before.

I was quite open with some of my female clients about my life and would often tell them about my son, his children and my desire to meet them one day. One of my clients who is also a friend, enquired as to what was stopping me from just getting onboard an airplane and going to meet him. It was hard for me to explain to her something that I myself could not totally understand. I just had an inner knowing that it was not the right time. My friend thought the reason was due to lack of finances, so she offered to pay for my flights. Even though I was touched deeply by her kindness, I knew not to take up her offer. I was confident that I was going to meet my son one day, and hopefully, his children. I did not know when and that was alright for now. By following my own crazy will and ways, I had gotten nowhere. So, I placed this whole situation into the hands of The Lord, knowing that I had to trust Him with it as His timing is always perfect.

In May 2016, I travelled to the south east coast of Africa to Mozambique, to volunteer in an orphanage in Pemba. One morning before sunrise, I was in one of the prayer huts praying and listening to see if God had anything to say to me. Just as the sun became visible on the horizon, I somehow had an inner knowing that He was communicating with me, asking me to write my story. I was overwhelmed and began making notes in my journal as He 'spoke' to me. He told me to write about how He was answering my prayer to find and meet my son and to speak of other events in my life so as to demonstrate His love, mercy and grace to all who choose to follow Jesus. God told me not to 'soften' my story or leave out specific details about my life, that to be honest, I would have preferred not to tell anyone about. I was surprised when I heard this and wondered if I had just made it all up in my imagination. But I instantly felt peaceful, and although I had not heard an audible voice, I knew that it was God communicating with me. I had started to write for my children's sake a few years ago when my mother first prompted me to do so, but I gave up after only a few pages, not really knowing what to say and also wondering, 'who would be interested in reading my story anyway'?

I was excited as I walked back to the room that I shared with five other female volunteers. When I reached our humble abode, I noticed the father of one of my roommates standing in the garden below. This man had already been such an encouragement to me, and I presumed he was waiting for his daughter. But he beckoned to me, so I walked down the pathway to meet with him. He seemed excited and told me he had just received a Word from God, asking him to give me a message. I was to write my story and not attempt to make it look as though my life was less harsh than it really had been. This was all the confirmation I needed. I told him that I had just had the very same Word while I was in the prayer hut only minutes before. Both of us were overwhelmed with joy, knowing that God had just expressed His will for me to both of us.

When I arrived home from Mozambique, I met a lady through my work whom I will call Cheryl, and we became good friends. I felt so comfortable when I was with her and we shared the ups and downs we had each experienced in our lives. One day, she told me she was going on a trip to visit some of her old acquaintances whom she caught up with at least once per year. As she spoke about this trip and how important it was for her to keep in touch with special people in her life, I began to feel guilty about not keeping in regular contact with my special childhood friend. Even though Lynne and I spoke to each other on the phone at least once or twice a year, this conversation with Cheryl was causing me to feel a little guilty. I suddenly felt an urgency to make more of an effort to contact Lynne and meet in person, after all these years. I expressed how I was feeling to my new friend. She asked me how long it had been since I'd seen Lynne. I was shocked when I realised that it was at least forty years.

Cheryl then enquired; 'Where does Lynne live? And what about that son of yours? When are you going to meet him? Where does he live'?

As I answered her questions, I realised that Lynne and my son resided within hours of each other.

Cheryl's next remark shocked me, to say the least. 'You and I are going on a road trip. Work out when it suits you and let me know. I am taking you to meet your son and to re-unite with your girlfriend'.

I felt fear and excitement all rolled in together. I had really been put me on the spot, but somehow it felt right. That night I looked at a couple of dates a few months out and messaged my son and my girlfriend separately, asking whether the days I had chosen would suit them for me to come and visit. I wondered in my heart if my son was ready for this.

I guess it was rather crazy of me to expect an immediate response, but I must admit I did. The next day when I had not heard from either of them, my mind became my worst enemy. I began making up stories in my head as to why my son would not want to meet me. I was not worried about not receiving a message from Lynne, because I knew she would jump at the chance of us getting together after so long. But I was concerned about my son and feared he may reject my invitation. I tried to undo what I had done by sending another message, saying that I realised it was short notice and that we could make it some other time. Within a couple of hours, I received a text confirming the dates suited and he looked forward to meeting me. Thank goodness he had completely ignored my previous message. I invited his partner to come too as not only did I wish to meet her but felt she would be a support for him. I spoke to my brother and his wife, telling them what was about to happen and asked if they would also like to be part of the meeting. From the day my brother found out he had another nephew years previously, he had longed to meet him. He and his wife were now thrilled at the prospect of this finally happening. Lynne replied to my message and expressed her excitement that we were going to see each other again after all this time

 I began worrying about how long it would take to drive to this destination and back, plus the expense of accommodation along the way. After discussing this with Cheryl, I decided it was easier and far less expensive, for both of us, if I booked a round trip by air to this meeting in Sydney, New South Wales. Her one request was that she drive me to the airport. She wanted to make sure I was going to go through with this and finally meet my son. I could now see the hand of God in everything since his birth, the heartache of losing him for the past forty-six and a half years, until now. This was in His perfect timing and I believe He had used Cheryl, to bring this about.

## Chapter Twenty-Five

## A Dream Come True

### —2016—

*'O LORD, You are my God;*
*I will exalt You,*
*I will praise and give thanks to Your name;*
*for You have done miraculous things,*
*Plans formed long, long ago,*
*[fulfilled] with perfect faithfulness'.*
—Isaiah 25:1 AMP—

I began counting down the days and spent most of the last six weeks imagining how it would be for both of us. The last time we had been together was forty-six and a half years ago, on the day he was born. I also looked forward to spending time with my brother, his wife and family and to reunite with Lynne and her husband, whom I had not seen since we were in our early 20s. As each day passed, I was more amazed at the way everything was falling into place. Dates that suited us all to meet, plane flights at discounted prices for the exact times I needed to travel, and of course, the way all of this had come about. The entire process had been in God's hands from start to finish. I was overwhelmed by His goodness and mercy.

On the 29th of September, 2016, Cheryl drove me to the airport, and to say I was excited would be an understatement. She was also excited. I was so grateful to her that she had been prompted to speak to me and give me the encouragement I so needed at the time. I do not know if she realised it or not, but God was using her as part of His plan.

It was wonderful to spend precious time with my family in Sydney, prior to meeting my son. My brother proudly showed me a completed copy of our 'family tree' which he had been working on for many years. He had spent hours researching our history and I appreciated him doing this, not only for his family's benefit, but also for my sisters and me and our families. The day prior to this very special meeting, my brother asked if I thought my son would be interested in having a copy of the family tree, as well as our grandfather's war records and some old photos of the farm I grew up on from 1952 till 1968. Our grandfather had written a diary whilst participating as a soldier in World War I. I was unsure about this, so we decided to prepare copies of these items, anyway, and take them with us the following day.

On the evening prior to the meeting, I was travelling with my brother and sister-in-law in their car, when my phone rang. I answered, and two very precious friends of mine greeted me excitedly. I could see them as they had 'face-timed' me. This couple open their home to a group of people each Friday night, where we share a meal together and have Bible study. I have been part of this 'family' for at least eight years. It just so happened that this was a Friday night, so the group were all there except for me. I had shared my story openly with them and they were aware that I was in Sydney to meet my son. They were praying for it all to go well for both of us, according to God's perfect plan. As they passed the phone from one to another, each person spoke words of encouragement. I was overwhelmed, not only by what they said, but their genuine love for me.

On the morning of the 1st of October, 2016, as I was rousing from sleep, I thought at first that I was waking from a dream. A dream that something wonderful was about to happen. But then I realised that this was the day I had awaited for so long. While I was preparing to leave, I began receiving many uplifting and encouraging messages from family and friends, and a song filled my heart. After all this time, I was finally going to meet my son.

I tried hard to contain my emotions as my brother and sister-in-law drove me to the arranged meeting place. I asked my brother along the way, that if an opportunity presented itself, would he try to discreetly take a photo of my son and me when we first met each other. I never ever wanted to forget that special moment. My brother explained that he would stay in the background so as not to intrude and if he could capture a photo or two without taking away from the moment, he would.

We found the restaurant where we had arranged to meet and I saw my son walking toward me. I recognised him from the photos I had seen. Words cannot explain the emotions I was feeling. When we embraced, I felt the exact same love for him I had when I held him ever so briefly on the day of his birth. We then moved to a table outside the restaurant and my son introduced me to his partner. It was as though I had been struck dumb. I was speechless. I thank God that my brother and his wife came to join us not long after we were seated. This was not part of the plan. They had come along to support me, but their idea was to casually join us for lunch, after we had spent some time together. It was amazing how this whole meeting was unfolding.

It was becoming more and more obvious to me that The Lord Himself was right there with us.

My brother introduced my sister-in-law and himself and they began a conversation with my son and his partner. I remained silent, still in shock and disbelief. I was trying hard not to stare at my son but wanting to at the same time. Prompted by a question or two from my brother, I finally found my voice. I savoured our conversation as we sat over lunch, listening intently to my son's every word. There were many questions we asked of each other in an attempt to find out as much as we could in the short time we had.

My brother told my son a little of our family history. How some of our relatives from as far back as the 1800s, had worked in similar (and in some cases the same) profession as my son. It is hard to conceive how our very DNA and the choices we make can affect generations back through time. My brother had also worked in the same occupation, years previously. It was fascinating to see the connections. There were noticeably clear and distinct similarities in interests and other aspects of not only *our* lives, but the lives of my daughters and their children, and my son's children. This was such a happy reunion, a special day I will never ever forget.

As our time together drew to an end, I plucked up the courage to ask my son if he would be interested in the family history items I had bought along? He eagerly accepted all of these. As we said our goodbyes, I was not sad about the fact that we had only spent a few hours together. I felt deep in my heart that this was just the beginning of a lifelong relationship between us. I found it hard to write about this, not because I was feeling emotionally overwhelmed, but because it was so surreal. I had waited for this day for forty-six and a half years. How does one explain an occasion so 'God ordained'? I give all the Glory to Him for bringing this about. It was as though He wrote the script, and we were the actors in a play.

The next day, I wrote the following in my diary:

*2/10/2016*
'I cannot describe how meeting him yesterday has brought about so much healing. God showed me a vision this morning of a human heart with a dark spot in the bottom of it. It was just a small spot, but then it suddenly was filled with healing light, and a totally restored heart transformed before my eyes. I am so in awe of what has just occurred in my life. The connection for the time we were together was supernatural to be sure. I believed in God for a wonderful reunion with my son, but I never believed just how awesome it truly would be. I cannot write down or describe what took place because it was from God. How can one describe His mighty Love, Goodness, Kindness, Grace, Restoration and Mercy for us'?

Lynne and her husband came to my family's home to visit the following day. They listened in awe as I briefly told them the story of what had taken place in my life since we had last been together and disclosed every minute detail of the meeting with my son. They were so happy for me. Lynne and I recalled quite a lot of things from our childhood. We reminisced about how we used to call each other 'kid'. Also, when Mum, Dad, my brother and I lived in a shed at the back of our block of land at the beach, whilst our house was being built. We recalled how Mum used to put a mattress under our dining table due to the lack of space in the shed for Lynne and me to sleep on whenever she stayed the night. She reminded me of her last sleepover and how we lay on the mattress whispering to each other so as not to keep the rest of my family awake. At the time I had just discovered I was pregnant and confided in her about how I needed to break the news to my mother. She had tried to console me as I cried myself to sleep.

Tears came to my eyes, when she revealed to me how her mum wanted to take me in after she heard of my predicament, all those years ago. But my parents had already asked me to leave home and nobody seemed to know where I had gone. It had all happened very quickly. I felt momentarily sad when I thought about what could have been. But my sadness soon turned to joy, as I remembered once more of the gift I had given a family who could not have children of their own.

Since the first meeting with my son, I have been fortunate enough to see him once again, along with two of my daughters. It was amazing and I just could not stop smiling as I observed three of my children together at last. I am so proud of him for who he is, and all that he has achieved in his life. I am eternally grateful to have a relationship with him and look forward to the day when his children and mine can finally meet one another.

## Chapter Twenty-Six

## Discovering Your Identity in Christ Jesus

*'For we are God's masterpiece. He has created us anew in Christ Jesus, so we can do the good things He planned for us long ago'.*

—**Ephesians 2:10 NLT**—

Not long after I invited Jesus to come and be my personal Lord and Saviour, I read a story in the Bible in the Gospel of John chapter 4, about Jesus' encounter with a woman from Samaria. This is an incredible story of how He touched not only *her* life, but many others in the city where she lived. The story goes something like this:

Jesus was in Judea and He needed to go to Galilee. The shortest way to His destination was to travel through the country of Samaria. Jesus was of Jewish decent and most Jewish people avoided Samaria due to ill feeling between the Jews and Samaritan people. But He obviously had no bias towards the Samaritans and chose to take this route. This more than likely was part of a divine plan for Him to meet a certain Samaritan woman.

He became weary from His long journey and sat down beside a well. It was not long before a woman came to draw water for her household. When Jesus asked her for a drink, she was puzzled as to why He would have anything to do with her, as she perceived that He was a Jewish man. He offered her 'living water' and explained that all who drink of this water, that He offers to everyone, will never thirst again. And the 'living water' will become in that person, a fountain springing up into everlasting life. The woman asked Jesus to give her the water so that she would never be thirsty. Then He revealed to her that He knew everything about her. He was even aware that she had been married five times and was currently living with a man. The woman was amazed and became even more so when He told her that He was in fact the Messiah. She believed what He said and ran and told people in her city all about her encounter with Jesus. Many came to see for themselves, then also believed. Jesus spent time with the Samaritan woman even though He knew of her sin. She was the very first person to whom He introduced Himself as the Messiah. He did not even give His own disciples this honour when He first called them.

Just like the woman from Samaria, I have been married several times and lived in de facto relationships with different men. Despite the addictive and destructive pattern that *was* my life, Jesus still desired to have an intimate relationship with me. He comes to save the lost, so He went out of His way to pursue me and accepted me regardless of my sin, just as He did the woman from Samaria

I was puzzled at first as to why He would want anything to do with me. But I realise now that He loves me and had been pursuing me the entire time, in order to set me totally free from the things in my life that were holding me captive. He never gave up in His pursuit, and eventually, He defeated my rebellion when I put my trust in Him. It was only then that realised I had finally discovered the man of my dreams. Jesus is passionate, polite and such a Gentleman that He never forces Himself on me. He allows me to make my own choices, even though He lovingly guides me to the ones He knows are for my higher good. He is outrageously generous, my best friend and the lover of my soul. His love is so great for me, that He gave up His life just so I could have mine.

Jesus also understands my suffering, as He also suffered while living on earth. His will was to forgive me and end once and for all, my senseless search for love and acceptance through temporal means that do not last. He had a plan and purpose for me and began to heal my brokenness so as to bring me into an amazing relationship with Him.

This was God's perfect plan for me all along, and it is His plan for all people. All we have to offer Him in exchange for His forgiveness, is our brokenness. He loves all mankind and especially had you in mind before the earth was even created. He wishes the absolute best for our lives. Perhaps you also can see similarities in the Samaritan woman's life prior to her meeting Jesus with your own.

God is the author of our lives if we allow Him to be. His story for all creation includes Him and is a love story of Eternal Hope and Redemption. Unfortunately, most of my life I edited the main character out of the story God originally wrote for me and chose to 'do life' my way. Finally, I realised that my story without God wasn't working and never would whilst *I* was in control.

**In Genesis 1:26, God says,**

> 'Let Us make man in Our image'.

We were created in the image of God, Jesus and the Holy Spirit. That means we are perfect. With this in mind, then, shouldn't we accept ourselves as He created us to be?? He sees you and me as a beautiful work of art, a masterpiece, even though we may think otherwise. God equips each and every person with unique talents and giftings, therefore, we already have everything we need to fulfil the destiny He has planned for us.

But how do we discover our identity and our reason for being on the earth? Are you like I was, not only without knowledge of what having an identity meant, but also not realising that God has a plan and purpose for your life? Maybe you think your identity is to be found in being a parent, how smart you are, your role at work, how much money you can stockpile in the bank, what you own already, how you look, or how fit you are or who others think you should be?

**But God says in Ephesians 2:10, that,**

> 'You are His masterpiece and that He has created you anew in Christ Jesus, so you can do the good things He planned for you long ago'.

You are unique and so special that no other person on earth, even has the same fingerprints as yours. And, in the same way that each person has different DNA, so are God's plans for each of our individual destinies.

So, why do we often feel inferior or not good enough? Are we doubting God's workmanship? He handcrafted you, and you are vital to His plans for all creation. And the 'good things' spoken of in this Scripture do not mean 'things done through our effort'. Doing 'good' won't get us to heaven. It means that by allowing Jesus to live His life through us, He can continue to do the 'good' He did on earth before He died and rose again. We are designed to continue His work and He has provided us with all we need, to fulfill His will.

**Firstly, I would like to give you some advice about how not to find your identity.** Don't compare yourself with others or rely on people to tell you who you are or how you should be. Don't allow other folks' reactions to you or their unkind words make you believe that you are anything less than what God intended for you to be. It must break His heart to witness His creation being mistreated. And in the same way, God doesn't like it when we are unkind to others.

**In 1 Corinthians 16:14, the Apostle Paul tells us,**

> 'Let all that you do be done with love'.

I allowed many people to use and abuse me until I was well into my fiftieth year, simply because I did not know who I was, or why I even existed. I thought I was ugly, useless and worthless. Please do not accept the unacceptable, as I did, in your relationships with other people. This is regardless of whether it is a relationship with your spouse, children, best friend, employer, teacher or whoever. I used to think that I deserved to be treated badly; that was until I found Jesus.

## How to Find Your Identity

God loves you and when you acknowledge *His* identity, you will discover your own. Let's look at what else He says about our identity in the Bible.

> 'Behold what manner of love the Father has bestowed on us,
> that we should be called children of God!'
> —1 John 3:1—

We are God's children and what He thinks about us is never based upon our own abilities, which means I no longer have to be someone else's idea of how I should be. I can be exactly, intricately, uniquely, wondrously the one-of-a-kind creation God purposed for me.

He often gives us little prompts along the way. For example, we may be reading the Bible, and suddenly words seem to just jump off the page. They may be words we have read before, but they weren't relevant to us at that particular time. Or God may bring people across our path to encourage us to fulfil His plan and purpose for our lives. And these people may or may not be aware that God is using them for our benefit. We might read a book or see a movie and be motivated by something striking that we read or witness, knowing for sure that it was God reaching out to us in this particular way. And sometimes we will fail to notice Him trying to get our attention and realise months or even years down the track that we missed an opportunity that had been placed before us.

All we need to do to step into our identity is to give our lives to Jesus in order to begin the journey that God purposed for us. He will reveal to you if certain people or things in your life are holding you back from becoming who He created you to be. It seemed for most of my life that I was 'in the world' but wanting so desperately to get 'out of the world'. I was lost, confused, sad and filled with fear. In order to escape the world, I used drugs, alcohol, meditation techniques, busyness, dysfunctional relationships, self-harming, bulimia and more. None of this worked as it was merely escapism. You might have resorted to similar things yourself. Or, just as I did, you may have known God but walked away from Him. But be rest assured that He has never taken His eyes off you and will draw near to you when you draw near to Him.

As I look back at my past and compare it to my present situation, the difference is so vast, that it is like looking at black and white. Black was my past; white is my future with God as Lord of my life. As a daughter of the King, I know my identity is in Him and how much He loves me. And I like who I have become since I put my trust in Jesus. I will never again accept the unacceptable in any relationship and will do my best to extend love to all people. I am so grateful to God for His unconditional love for me and how He has turned my life around. I simply take each day as it comes now, knowing He is in control and will lead me and provide for me through my faith in Him.

God wants us to surrender our lives, along with our self-sufficiency, to Him. Only then can we escape the bondage of Satan who wants us as his possession, and whose intention is to steal, kill and destroy mankind. Because of how much I love God, I do not find it difficult to give every aspect of my life to Him. Instead of looking to others for my sense of self-worth and acceptance, I now look to God. And when I do this, He reflects back to me exactly how much He loves me and reminds me of who He says I am. God loves you so much that He came to earth in the form of a man, Jesus Christ, and willingly died on a cross, so that you could be set free from the chains of Satan that bind you. Please, please, please, give your life to Jesus, discover your precious identity in Him and His purpose for your life, and as a child of God, never again allow anyone to treat you badly.

> 'Behold, children are a heritage from the Lord'.
>
> —Psalm 127:3—

Dear God,
I have left it a little late to teach my children about You, but I trust that by reading my story of the miraculous ways You worked in my life, that they and their partners, their children and their children's children and any future generations, will come to know You also, by inviting You to be their Lord and Saviour as I did. I ask that You bless them with the knowledge and revelation of who You are and show them the plans and purposes You desired for them before You created the earth. In Jesus Name I ask this. Amen.

> 'Whereas you do not know what will happen tomorrow. For what is your life? It is even a vapor that appears for a little time and then vanishes away'.
>
> —James 4:14—

# Chapter Twenty-Seven

## A Love Letter from God

*'For God so loved the world that He gave
His only begotten Son,
That whoever believes in Him should not perish
but have everlasting life'.*

—John 3:16—

I sincerely believe God wrote a love letter and placed it in my heart, the contents of which were never meant for me to keep to myself but to share with you. His desire is for me to tell you about Him in this book and to let you know how much he loves you. If you already know Jesus, you know what I am talking about. My prayer is, that because you have read about God's love, kindness, mercy and grace toward me, you will be convinced that He feels the same way about you.

When God originally created the world, it represented His perfect design. He made people in His image who lived with Him in peace, love and unity until sin entered and separated them from God and His perfect plan. God hates sin and He does not wish for anyone to suffer its penalty.

**Romans 6:23** tells us,

> 'For the wages of sin is death, but the gift of God is eternal life in Christ Jesus our Lord'.

Without God in their lives to lead and guide them, the world became a broken place and even though some people tried to do good, they could not succeed by themselves. This was the total opposite of what God had originally planned. People rebelled against Him and became selfish, confused, angry and filled with fear as they tried to make their own way through life. It is still the same today. Many still die in their broken state only to be separated from God for eternity.

Because of His great love for us, God did not wish to leave us in our brokenness. His desire was to save us. To reconcile us with Himself, once again. That is why He came to earth as a human in the form of Jesus and willingly took all of our sin upon Himself, suffering and dying on a cross in our place. His plan is to redeem us; Satan's plan is to deceive us.

In **2 Corinthians 4:4**, the Apostle Paul tells us that 'the god of this age', Satan, has blinded the minds of unbelievers so that they cannot see the light of the Gospel message. Jesus gave His own life as a substitution for every mistake we have ever made. When He died and rose again victorious through the power of God, He took all of your sin and mine and cancelled it, once and for all. There is no greater love than this. Jesus gave His life so we could have ours. In Jesus' death, He dealt with our disobedience. In His resurrection, He gave us Life. Jesus is the only way humans can be reunited with God, our heavenly Father. When He came into the world, He was despised, rejected and persecuted by many, and nothing much has changed even to this day. But despite this, He willingly stood in our place and battled our enemy, Satan.

If we turn from our sin and make Jesus our Lord and Saviour, we come back into relationship with God and His original design and plan for our lives. God is our Heavenly Father, our Spiritual Father, and is a Holy God who loves us deeply. Satan tries to make us believe that all we need do, in order to get to Heaven, is to be a 'good person' and live our lives in our own strength. I also used to believe this. Others believe they need to clean up their lives *before* coming to Jesus. He died for us while we were still enslaved to sin. His sacrifice wasn't dependent on *our* performance. He accepts us just as we are, in all our brokenness.

We were never meant to just be born, live our lives, then die. What would be the point of that? There is a Spiritual Life available to us if we choose to accept it. In the Gospel of **John 14:6**, Jesus said,

'I am the way, the truth, and the life'.

Even though other religious hierarchy of Jesus' time (and sometimes even His own disciples and family,) disagreed with Him because of the way He was, He took no notice. He was about His Father God's business, and by being in the company of 'the lost', He radically transformed their lives. He takes time to spend with those whom others have given up on long ago as a 'lost cause'. Jesus sees the best in everybody.

God pursues us and loves us so much that He wants to bless us with the gift of eternal life, so that we will be with Him forever, even after our mortal body gives up and passes from this world. But He has also given us 'free will'. That means we can either accept the gift or make an excuse not to receive it. Eternal life is a never-ending relationship with God the Father and God the Son and is available to all who trust in Him. Often, we are so busy with life, that we think we don't have time for the eternal Lover of our souls, instead preferring to try to work out our own destiny. True freedom, though, is not to turn away from our Creator, but instead, to walk with Him. God wants us to surrender our lives to Him, but He will never force us. The choice is ours. Whatever our choice, ultimately, we are choosing our own destiny.

**In the Gospel of Mathew 7:13-14 Jesus says,**

> 'Enter by the narrow gate; for wide is the gate and broad is the way that leads to destruction, and there are many who go in by it. Because narrow is the gate and difficult is the way which leads to life, and there are few who find it'.

Please, I beg of you. Surrender your life to Jesus, because it is through Him that we come to God. You will more than likely be persecuted for doing so and may think, 'Why would I do this if persecution is the price I will pay?' But if we do not surrender our lives to God and accept the wonderful gift of Salvation, our alternative is to die and live in eternal damnation in hell. Don't reject this gift of life and remain enslaved to Satan. Instead, come and experience God's liberating love for you and walk into freedom.

Sometimes fear will try to stop us. Fear of failure, fear of being criticised, fear of change. Fear is Satan's way of holding us back from what God wants us to step into and is the opposite of love. Love sets you free. While we are not walking with God, we are oppressed by Satanic rule, whether we are aware of this or not. We are all sinners and we need a saviour, and Jesus is that saviour.

**John 3:36** says,

> 'He who believes in the Son has everlasting life; and he who does not believe the Son shall not see life, but the wrath of God abides on him'.

In **John 10:27,28** Jesus said,

> 'My sheep hear My voice, and I know them, and they follow Me. And I give them eternal life, and they shall never perish; neither shall anyone snatch them out of my hand'.

Through scripture, God is talking to us and inviting us all to come by faith to Jesus and accept His gracious offer of eternal life. One day,

Jesus is coming back for those of us who have given our lives to Him, unless we have departed from this earth and are already in His presence. In order to come into an intimate relationship with God, we must first look at four important things we need to do:

**1. Confess that we are sinners.** That we have fallen short of God's perfect standard. God has compassion for us and wants us to live and not die. He took all our sin so that anyone who believes in Him can be forgiven. But we must also forgive all who have ever hurt us.

In **Mathew 6:14-15** Jesus said,

'For if you forgive men their trespasses, your heavenly Father will also forgive you. But if you do not forgive men their trespasses, neither will your Father forgive your trespasses'.

**2. Believe that Jesus is the Son of God.** He willingly died on a cross for us so that our sins could be forgiven. God raised Him from the dead and He is alive today.

In **Romans 5:8,** the apostle Paul tells us,

'But God demonstrates His own love toward us, in that while we were still sinners, Christ died for us'.

This was how God resolved the issue of serious sin for us all.

**3. Repent of our sin.** Repentance is a change of heart and mind that brings us closer to God. Our desire to repent is motivated by our love for Him and a sincere desire to give our lives to Him. We must be sorry, ask God to forgive us, and with the help of the Holy Spirit, turn from all known sin and begin doing what is right. He has chosen us to be His children and is waiting for us to respond to His call on our life. Stop running *from* God and instead, run *to* Him.

Jesus said in **Luke 5:32,**

'I have not come to call the righteous, but sinners, to repentance'.

And in Luke 13:3 He said,

> 'But unless you repent, you will all likewise perish'.

Repentance is necessary to receive the new life Jesus offers us.

**4. Invite Jesus to be your Lord and Saviour.** We must receive Jesus into our lives in order to be saved. When we give our lives to Him, we move from the position of knowing about God to knowing God personally.

In **Luke 19:10** Jesus said;

> 'For the Son of Man came to seek and to save the lost'.

When we invite Jesus to be our Lord and Saviour, we come back into relationship with God, and He then looks upon us as He looks at the One who surrounds us, and that one is Jesus. God then sees us as blameless, shameless, righteous and holy.

In the book of **Mathew 11:28-30** Jesus says:

> 'Come to Me, all you who labor and are heavy laden, and I will give you rest. Take My yoke upon you and learn from Me, for I am gentle and lowly in heart, and you will find rest for your souls. For My yoke is easy and My burden is light'.

We come into a beautiful relationship and friendship with Jesus when we invite Him into our hearts. He comes and lives there permanently. If you would like to receive Jesus as your very own personal Lord and Saviour, all you need do is ask God in faith today through the following prayer:

'Dear Lord Jesus,

I believe that you are the Son of God and I choose to accept Your free gift of Eternal life. Thank you for dying on a cross for me, so that all of my sin could be forgiven and my relationship with God can be restored. I am genuinely sorry for sinning against You, and I ask You today to please forgive me and help me to turn away from any and all future sin. Please come and live within my heart today. I now put my trust in You to take over every area of my life and be my personal Lord and Saviour. May Your will be done, now and forever more. Amen'.

In **Romans 10:13**, the apostle Paul says,

'For whoever calls on the name of the LORD shall be saved'.

I am so happy that you have just prayed this prayer. God is passionate to save His children, and when we give our life to Jesus, every single activity in heaven stops so a celebration can begin. The angels are rejoicing right now because you have turned to God in repentance and faith. God has wiped your slate completely clean of sin. You are a redeemed child of His and this is your identity through God's Spirit which now abides within you. He will be present with you for the rest of your life on earth. Nothing can prevent you now from becoming everything He intends you to be. Because you have given your life to Jesus, He gives Himself to you.

In **1 John 4:15**, John says,

'Whoever confesses that Jesus is the Son of God, God abides in him, and he in God'.

So you will not feel alone on this new and exciting journey you have just embarked upon, find a Christian church where you can come into fellowship with other believers who will encourage you along the way. Spend time with the Lord each day, reading His Word, resting in His Holy Presence and praying. You can talk to God about everything, anywhere, just as you would a best friend. After all, that is what He is. And do not forget to tell others about Him and how much He loves them also.

**Proverbs 3:5-6** says,

> 'Trust in the LORD with all your heart, and lean not on your own understanding; In all your ways acknowledge Him, and He shall direct your paths'.

Give Him all your goodness as well as your brokenness then press into the future, not allowing your past to hold you back. I believe in God's promises and that He desires for everyone to take possession of what He has promised. After all, aren't we, as children of God, co-heirs with Jesus? As I reflect on God's goodness in my life, I find myself almost bursting with love for Him. My desire is to surrender myself to Him totally, so He can use me to fulfil His purposes and plans for His Glory on the earth, until He calls me home. I love spending as much time as I can each day in His Holy Presence.

In the book of **James 4:8**, James says,

> 'Draw near to God and He will draw near to you'.

Jesus wants you to give Him all of your cares. In **1 Peter 5:7**, Peter says,

> 'Casting all your care upon Him, for He cares for you'.

In the very next verse, he warns us to be aware, though, that the devil (Satan) is very real and we must be wide awake to the fact that he will want to harm us, attempting to draw us back into sin, so he can distract us from our walk with the Lord.

Jesus said in **John 10:10**,

> 'The thief does not come except to steal, and to kill, and to destroy. I have come that they may have life, and that they may have *it* more abundantly'.

Fortunately, when we put our faith in Jesus, we have the living God, our Lord and Saviour to keep and protect us from Satan. Christians are not immune to temptation, however, but Jesus understands our weakness in this area, as He also was tempted just like us.

**1 Corinthians 10:13** says that,

> 'No temptation has overtaken you except such as is common to man; but God is faithful, who will not allow you to be tempted beyond what you are able, but with the temptation will also make the way of escape, that you may be able to bear it'.

Now that you have become a Christian, begin to prepare for eternity, where you will live with Jesus forever.

The apostle Paul tells us in **2 Corinthians 4:18**,

> 'While we do not look at the things which are seen, but at the things which are not seen. For the things which are seen *are* temporary, but the things which are not seen *are* eternal'.

What better way than to spend each day with Almighty God as He begins to change you by the power of His love. He will gradually heal the pieces of your brokenness and weave them into a beautiful tapestry, as you look on in sheer wonderment, at His transforming power in your life.

God showed me a vision this morning. It was as a picture in a frame. At the top of the picture was a mighty light. In front of the light, but not hiding the light, was a massive mountain. God is the light. He told me that no matter what mountains we face in our lives, whether they be fear, sickness, disease, relationship breakdowns, addictions, grief etc., look to the light. Look above the mountain to Him. Turn your eyes upon Jesus and all else will pale in comparison. When you put your faith in Him, the comfort, peace, strength and love He will lavish upon you as you go *through* the storms of life will cause the mountains to crumble and fall away. Yes, the storms of life will come and go but will not overwhelm you now that you have Jesus as your Lord and Saviour.

### The Safety of Abiding in the Presence of God

*He who dwells in the secret place of the Most High*
*Shall abide under the shadow of the Almighty.*
*I will say of the LORD, 'He is my*
*refuge and my fortress;*
*My God, in Him I will trust'.*

—Psalm 91:1-2—

## THE END

# Epilogue

I can hardly believe four years have passed since I began to write my story. It has been an incredible journey. Although it was hard at times to go back to my past, relive it and admit the mistakes I had made, it has served to remind me of how God supernaturally intervenes in our lives. May He receive all the glory for this. It is only by His grace, love and mercy through our Lord Jesus, that I have come this far. It truly was a dream come true when I first met my son and his fiancé in 2016. Two of my daughters and I have met with him since, and my family and I look forward to spending more time with him and meeting his three adult children.

For the past two years I have resided in a retirement village, renting a small one-bedroom unit. I am eternally grateful for this peaceful retreat. I give thanks as I walk on tree lined paths within the village at daybreak, bypassing kangaroos and listening as the dawn chorus of birds welcome the new day.

I spend most of my time these days with family, catching up with friends, fishing, playing my violin and attending church. I still love to exercise and eat healthy food, but no longer am obsessive about either. I enjoy taking long walks on the beach, visiting our beautiful islands just off the coast and going sailing occasionally. Being mindful of course, due to my past experience. At the moment, I am praying for opportunities to share my story face to face with people who feel they have no hope. I wish to encourage those who are, or have been, victims of abuse or suffering in other ways. May God's will be done in my life.

    I would like to give thanks to my family and friends, for encouraging me in everything I do. Also, I am forever grateful to God through the Lord Jesus, for turning my life around and filling my heart to overflowing with love and compassion for others. I do not have a clear picture of what His plans are for me as yet, but what I do know, is that all I need is in Him. Whatever happens next as a result of me writing my story, I will keep a diary as I have always done and may even decide to write another 'Love letter'. I have more peace and joy at this present time than I have ever experienced before in my life, and my prayer is that you can also have this. I pray that you have been blessed, by reading my story.

*'The Lord bless you and keep you.*
*The Lord make His face shine upon you,*
*and be gracious to you.*
*The Lord lift up His countenance upon you,*
*And give you peace'.*

**—Numbers 6:24-26 —**

www.ingramcontent.com/pod-product-compliance
Lightning Source LLC
Chambersburg PA
CBHW070251010526
44107CB00056B/2419